MICROSOFT CERTIFIED SYSTEMS ENGINEER

MCSE Windows® 2000 Network Administration Lab Manual

MICROSOFT CERTIFIED SYSTEMS ENGINEER

MCSE Windows® 2000 Network Administration Lab Manual

Nick LaManna

McGraw-Hill/Osborne
New York Chicago San Francisco
Lisbon London Madrid Mexico City Milan
New Delhi San Juan Seoul Singapore Sydney Toronto

McGraw-Hill/Osborne
2600 Tenth Street
Berkeley, California 94710
U.S.A.

To arrange bulk purchase discounts for sales promotions, premiums, or fund-raisers, please contact McGraw-Hill/Osborne at the above address. For information on translations or book distributors outside the U.S.A., please see the International Contact Information page immediately following the index of this book.

MCSE Windows® 2000 Network Administration Lab Manual

1234567890 CUS CUS 01987654321

ISBN 0-07-222302-2

Publisher	**Senior Project Editor**	**Production and Editorial**
Brandon A. Nordin	Betsy Manini	**Services**
		Anzai!, Inc.
Vice President & Associate	**Acquisitions Coordinator**	
Publisher	Athena Honore	**Series Designer**
Scott Rogers		Roberta Steele
	Technical Editor	
Acquisitions Editor	David Field	**Cover Series Designer**
Chris Johnson		Greg Scott

This book was composed with Corel VENTURA™ Publisher.

I want to thank my wonderful wife Jane and daughter Amanda
for their support and understanding over the course of this project.
Ciao, Babbo.

ABOUT THE AUTHOR

Nicola (Nick) LaManna, M.Ed., is currently the associate department chair for Information Technology, and assistant professor at New England Institute of Technology, based in Warwick, Rhode Island. He has worked in various positions in the computer-networking field for approximately 12 years. He completed training in Novell Netware Engineering, and was employed as a network administrator at Johnson and Wales University in Providence, Rhode Island.

After completing his Master of Education Degree in Information Technology from J & W, he began his teaching career as an adjunct with the university. Holding various teaching positions in the area, he accepted a position at New England Institute of Technology in 1998, where he currently focuses on networking.

Nick has worked on various texts for McGraw-Hill/Osborne as a technical editor, and reviewer. He continues to keep current with industry changes and standards, including Microsoft Windows 2000 and Novell NetWare 5.1 Certification courses.

Nick lives in Warwick, Rhode Island, with his lovely wife of 22 years, Jane, daughter Amanda, and faithful dog, Gremlin. He enjoys hiking in the mountains, cycling, and travel.

CONTENTS

ACKNOWLEDGMENTS

As this is my first formal venture into the publishing world, I would like to thank the following people:

- The great hard-working team at McGraw-Hill/Osborne, and to Chris Johnson and Athena Honore, for their patience and encouragement.
- To Lee Musick, Tom Anzai, and the rest of the Anzai! Inc. team for turning a manuscript into a polished product.
- To Dave Field, for his technical editing expertise and for catching those overlooked mistakes.

INTRODUCTION

Welcome to the *MCSE Windows 2000 Network Administration Lab Manual.* This lab manual is meant to complement the *MCSE Windows 2000 Network Administration Study Guide (Exam 70-216).* Skills needed to deploy and manage Windows 2000 networking components are reinforced with real-world lab exercises for each of the certification objectives. A prerequisite to successfully accomplish the intended learning outcomes of this lab manual is an exposure to Windows 2000 Professional and Windows 2000 Server software.

In This Lab Manual   This lab manual provides the necessary exposure and training to install, configure, manage, monitor, and troubleshoot a Windows 2000 network. Topics that are covered include the use and manipulation of standard networking protocols and Windows 2000 Server services, such as:

- Domain Naming Service (DNS)
- Dynamic Host Configuration Protocol (DHCP)
- Routing and Remote Access Services (RRAS)
- Windows Internet Naming Service (WINS)
- IP Routing
- Internet Connection Service (ICS)
- Network Address Translation (NAT)
- Microsoft Certificate Services

Each chapter also includes a lab analysis test and a key term quiz. Solutions for each chapter are also provided for comparison. After the completion of this lab manual, you will have a better understanding of a Windows 2000 networking infrastructure, and be capable of managing its daily operations.

Lab Exercises

Understanding the theory behind networking and Windows 2000 server principles is important for a network administrator. The question is, can you transfer this knowledge to a system situation? Each exercise allows you to apply and practice a particular concept or skill in a real-world scenario.

Case Studies   Each certification objective is presented as a case study. They provide a conceptual opportunity to apply your newly developed knowledge.

Learning Objectives   Working hand-in-hand with the study guide, one objective is to help you pass the certification exam. The second objective is to have you develop critical thinking. In networking, not all installations, re-installations, or network and system problems present themselves in the same fashion each time. To this end, you need to be able to analyze, consider your options and the result of each option, select and implement that option. If it works, great; if it doesn't, you start over again.

Lab Materials and Setup   To fully accomplish each lab, it is necessary that the following hardware and software requirements be met. If this is not possible, read through the steps and become familiar with the procedures as best you can.
   Windows 2000 Professional workstation:

- 64MB RAM
- Pentium 133 MHz or higher
- VGA monitor or better
- Mouse or other pointing device
- 12× or faster CD-ROM
- One or more hard drive with a minimum of 4GB free space
- Network card with either a BNC (coaxial cable) or CAT5 connection
- Dial-up or LAN connection (optional)

Windows 2000 Server:

- 128MB of RAM
- Pentium 133 MHz or higher

- VGA monitor or better
- Mouse or other pointing device
- 12× or faster CD-ROM
- One or more hard drive with a minimum of 4GB free space
- Network card with either a BNC (coaxial cable) or CAT5 connection
- Dial-up or LAN connection (optional)

The computers can be connected using a small network hub.

Getting Down-to-Business   The hands-on portion of each lab is step-by-step, not click-by-click. Step-by-steps provide explanations and instructions walking you through each task relevant to the certification exam.

Lab Analysis Test

These are short to medium-answer questions to quickly assess your comprehension of what you've learned in the study guide and each lab in the chapter. The answers should be in your own words. This shows that you've synthesized the information and you have a comprehensive understanding of the key concepts.

Key Term Quiz

These are technical words that you should be able to recognize and know their definitions and purpose. This will help you with the exam and on the job.

Solutions

Each chapter provides solutions for the Lab Exercises, the Lab Analysis Test, and the Key Term Quiz. These solutions are meant to compare your lab procedures, answers, or definitions, with the correct lab procedures, answers, or definitions. Those who may be familiar with Windows 2000 will find that there is more than one way to accomplish the step in certain parts of the lab exercises. The main objectives are understanding the processes and reaching the end result.

MICROSOFT CERTIFIED SYSTEMS ENGINEER

MCSE Windows® 2000
Network Administration
Lab Manual

MICROSOFT CERTIFIED SYSTEMS ENGINEER

1

Introduction to Implementing and Administering a Windows 2000 Network

LAB EXERCISES

Microsoft Windows 2000 provides many networking features and services found in Windows NT 4.0 and expands those features to include additional new and useful items. These new features include:

■ Active Directory Services (ADS)

■ Enhanced security

■ IP security (IPSec)

■ Plug and Play support

In this chapter, through word problems, we'll review some basic networking principles that include networking protocols: TCP/IP, NWLink, and NetBEUI. We'll look at a major networking model, the OSI model, and Internet Protocol (IP) addressing scheme.

LAB EXERCISE 1.01

Improving Networking Performance with Networking Protocols

15 Minutes

Your consulting firm has sent you to Costume Jewelry International to inspect its TCP/IP network and resolve a performance issue. Costume Jewelry's general manager is complaining that the network is slow and it's affecting productivity. The company's network consists of a Windows 2000 domain with four domain controllers, 800 Windows 2000 Professional workstations, and 5 Macintosh computers that connect to one server occasionally. As you inspect the network you discover they've added the following protocols to each server:

■ Services for Macintosh (Appletalk)

■ NWLink

■ NetBEUI

■ TCP/IP

What would your recommendation be for improving network performance?

Learning Objectives

In this lab you'll identify elements that affect network performance. By the end of this lab, you'll be able to:

■ Analyze a network and identify reasons for its slow performance

■ Identify ways to improve network performance

Lab Materials and Setup

For this lab exercise, you will need:

■ Pencil and paper

■ Windows 2000 Server

Getting Down to Business

When performing any problem-solving task, you want to approach it from a flow chart perspective. This means you want to systematically address each component of the problem.

Step 1.   Your first step is to analyze the problem. In the space below, describe the steps you should take when analyzing the problem. What are the things that may affect network performance?

_____

_____

Step 2.   Next, you need to implement a solution. In the space below write down the things you can do to solve the problem?

_____

_____

Step 3.   Finally, what steps can you take to ensure that your solutions works?

_____

_____

LAB EXERCISE 1.02

Using the OSI Model to Send an E-mail

15 Minutes

Sending information from one computer to another is more complicated than one thinks. This model defines a networking framework for implementing protocols in seven layers. Each layer interacts only with the layer immediately beneath it, and provides facilities for use by the layer above it. Protocols enable a layer in one host to interact with a corresponding layer in a remote host. Because this model is an "open standards," it is platform independent.

A user sending an e-mail message to a friend or business colleague only sees the top component involved in sending that e-mail. Consider this scenario: Ralph, who lives in a retirement village in Naples, Florida, composes and sends e-mail to his friend Norton who is retired in Phoenix, Arizona.

Learning Objectives

In this lab you'll get a better understanding of the OSI model. By the end of this lab, you'll be able to:

- Describe components of the OSI model
- Describe the function of each OSI layer

Lab Materials and Setup

For this lab exercise, you will need:

- Pencil and paper
- Windows 2000 Server

Getting Down to Business

In this lab exercise, we divide up the OSI model concept. First, identify each layer and then provide a description and/or function of each.

Step 1.   In the space below, describe which components of the OSI model are involved in transmitting that e-mail.

_____

_____

Step 2.   In the space below, describe the functions each OSI layer provides as Ralph's e-mail passes through the system.

_____

_____

LAB EXERCISE 1.03

Applying Internet Protocol (IP) Addressing   10 Minutes

Giovanni, a user from the international sales division, calls you to report that he is having trouble connecting to resources on the Windows 2000 domain. When asked, he provides additional information. He reveals that he is trying to connect to a server in San Diego. Other users in the department can connect to the server, but he can't. You also know that the computers have static IP addresses and have recently been reconfigured and upgraded.

Learning Objectives

In this lab you'll get your first exposure in identifying appropriate subnet masking. By the end of this lab, you'll be able to:

- Provide an educated solution to a TCP/IP protocol addressing problem
- Understand the purpose of subnet masking
- Understand the various addressing classes and ranges.

Lab Materials and Setup

For this lab exercise, you will need:

- Pencil and paper
- Windows 2000 Server

Getting Down to Business

Here's your first chance at working through an IP address problem. This shows that a misplaced number in the IP address or mask can mean the difference between connecting or not connecting to the network.

cross
Reference

Check section on IP addressing in Chapter 1 of the **Windows 2000 Network Administration Study Guide** *for help with the steps in this lab exercise.*

Step 1. In the space below, describe what you suspect the problem with his IP address configuration to be?

_____

_____

Step 2. In Giovanni's TCP/IP properties, you view his IP address to be 192.153.64.12, but his subnet mask is 255.255.0.0. Which class range is his IP address in, and what should his subnet mask be set at?

_____

_____

LAB ANALYSIS TEST

1. What is a Network Infrastructure?

_____

_____

2. How would you define Network Protocols?

_____

_____

3. How did the TCP/IP protocol suite come to be developed?

_____

_____

4. List and explain the TCP/IP utilities you would use to verify and test a TCP/IP configuration?

_____

_____

5. What benefits are provided to DNS clients from the dynamic update feature of Windows 2000?

_____

_____

KEY TERM QUIZ

Use the following vocabulary terms to complete the sentences below. Not all of the terms will be used. Definitions for these terms can be found in the *MCSE Windows 2000 Network Administration Study Guide.*

     Enhanced security

     IP addressing

     Plug and Play

     Subnet mask

     IP security (IPSec)

     Active directory

     Domain

     Open Systems Interconnection (OSI) model

     NetBEUI

     NWLink

1. The ability of an operating system to automatically detect and install device drivers is a support feature known as _____.

2. A _____ is a 32-bit number used to determine the portion of an IP address that represents the network ID and the host ID.

3. _____ is the 32-bit number address used to identify a host on a TCP/IP network.

4. Increased security measures, also known as _____, is available in Windows 2000 with the addition of Kerberos and IP security.

5. A container in the DNS name hierarchy that organizes components on the network is known as a/an _____.

LAB WRAP-UP

This chapter has provided a very brief introduction to networking and the concepts involved with a network infrastructure. We looked at networking protocols that affect a network's connection and performance, and how subnet masks determine appropriate network segments. Understanding the OSI model is necessary since it is the platform independent system that allows for interaction between a user, an application, and internal and external physical components.

LAB SOLUTIONS FOR CHAPTER 1

In this section, you'll find solutions to the Lab Exercises, Lab Analysis Test, and Key Term Quiz.

Lab Solution 1.01

Step 1.   It's quite obvious that the network has unnecessary protocols installed on the servers. Since the majority of clients on the network are Windows 2000 clients, it's not necessary to have any additional protocols installed.

Step 2.   You should remove NWLink, and NetBEUI from all servers. Remove the Macintosh service from all servers except for the server to which the Macintosh computers connect.

Step 3.   Just by removing these extra configurations from the servers, network performance will increase because fewer protocols are contending for network time.

   The above solution is the most direct and simple. Actually, depending on the binding order at the clients, some protocols may never be used. The client will use the first common protocol in its binding order to contact the server, and the server will respond with the same protocol. If that happens, the other protocols may not interfere with the network's performance. It is possible that TCP/IP is the only protocol used, in spite of all the protocols installed. A mixed client environment would cause difficulty in troubleshooting such a protocol-laden mess, especially with network monitoring tools.

Lab Solution 1.02

Answering these questions is fairly easy. All seven layers of the OSI model are used. What each layer's responsibility is, is more involved. Each layer plays a specific role when sending the e-mail. None of the layers are left out or skipped over. If one of the layers were to default or not provide service, then the transfer of information would terminate and you would have to retransmit.

Step 1.

- Application
- Presentation
- Session
- Transport
- Network
- Data Link
- Physical

Step 2.   When the e-mail is sent, it travels from the top to the bottom of the model. When the e-mail is received, it travels in reverse—from the bottom up.

- **Application**   interacts with user, provides services to applications and other network and software elements.
- **Presentation**   transforms data into the form that the application layer can accept. This layer also formats and encrypts data to be sent across a network.
- **Session**   establishes, manages, and terminates connections between applications.
- **Transport**   provides transfer of data between end systems, or hosts, and is responsible for point-to-point error recovery and flow control.
- **Network**   creates logical paths for transmitting data from one computer to another. It also handles congestion control and packet sequencing.
- **Data Link**   handles data packets by encoding and decoding them into bits. It also handles errors that may arise in the physical layer, controls flow of information and frame transmission.
- **Physical**   conveys the stream of electrical impulses through the network at the electrical and mechanical level.

Lab Solution 1.03

Step 1. Based on the information given, you determine that it is a TCP/IP protocol problem. If he had been able to connect to some resources or the problem was division wide, then it would be more of a network connectivity problem that would involve other routing equipment.

Step 2. Looking at Giovanni's TCP/IP properties window, you notice that the subnet mask of 255.255.0.0 is incorrect—this is a class B range mask. The IP address is a class C range address (first octet set between 192 – 223). His subnet mask should be 255.255.255.0. The purpose of a subnet mask is to identify the network address apart from the host address. The number 255 serves that purpose. In this case, the company's network ID is 192.153.64.0. The last octet set identifies the host's address, which will range from 1 to 254.

ANSWERS TO LAB ANALYSIS TEST

1. A network infrastructure is an internal set of physical and logical elements necessary for a network to function and exist. The physical components include the machines, cables, network cards, hubs, etc., all the tangibles. The logical components include the network protocols, DNS services, DHCP services, remote access, security protocols, etc., all the intangibles.

2. A network protocol is an agreed-upon language used between two computers that communicate on a network. The protocol defines how that information is transmitted, and how it is fragmented into small packets for transport over the network.

3. TCP/IP was the birth child of the U.S. Defense Advanced Research Projects Agency (DARPA) in 1973 to investigate techniques and technologies for interlinking packet networks of various kinds. They needed a way to let networked computers communicate transparently. Its real intended purpose was to provide government installations with a communications vehicle that would survive in case of a nuclear disaster.

   - **IPCONFIG** grabs TCP/IP configuration information on a computer.
   - **NETSTAT** shows protocol information and present connections.
   - **NBSTAT** displays local NetBIOS information.
   - **NSLOOKUP** finds the IP address or hostname of a machine.

- **ROUTE** shows a network's local routing table.
- **TRACERT** traces the path a packet takes, from the source to its destination.
- **PING** helps confirm connectivity on a network.
- **ARP** resolves IP addresses.

The dynamic update feature enables DNS client computers to register and automatically update their resource records with a DNS server whenever there is a change to that computer's information. This feature reduces the need to manually administer zone records, especially for clients that move or change locations on a regular basis and use a DHCP service to obtain an IP address.

ANSWERS TO KEY TERM QUIZ

1. Plug and play

2. Subnet mask

3. IP addressing

4. Enhanced security

5. Domain

2

The Domain Naming System: Introductory Concepts and Procedures

Y ou pick up the phone and call a number. This phone number contains an area code, prefix, and customer number (401-555-1212), not too unlike an *IP address (192.168.32.15)*. Your call is connected. The phone company logs your phone number, (area code-prefix-number), into their database having made that phone call (*your IP address*) which allows you to travel over the network. If you don't recall the phone number of the person or company you're calling, what do you do? You look in a phone book, such as the white pages or yellow pages (*search engine*). If you've called the number before and don't remember it, you look in your personal phone directory that lists the person or company alphabetically (*bookmarks or favorites*). Or, you've programmed the number into your phone's memory and just press speed-dial (*pull down menu in the URL field*).

DNS provides such a service. It's when you call directory assistance for someone's phone number. It resolves a web site's (*host*) name entered in the URL field of your browser to the site's IP address.

In this chapter, you'll practice setting up DNS services. First you'll install the services on your server. Then, you'll need to configure a root server and create the first zone. You'll also need to create a second standard primary forward and reverse lookup zone. Lastly, you'll create a delegated zone that will handle name-to-IP address resolutions.

LAB EXERCISE 2.01

Installing DNS and Zone File for First Time   10 Minutes

Your company, Big-bITe Consultants, has sent you to San Antonio, Texas to help South-of-the-Border Importers set up their DNS. The company, which imports food products from Mexico and South America, employs 1,500 employees in three buildings. They wish to use their intranet to give their employees access to personal payroll information, check stub information, yearly deductions and earnings, access to their benefits status, sick time and vacation time balances, medical insurance information, and so on.

Your first task is to install the DNS component of Windows 2000 and set up a primary DNS zone for the company's headquarters building. Your IT service manager has faxed the company's HR director, Ida Dewnought-Gnow, a profile form. You have the following information from that form:

IP address of server	192.128.32.01
Subnet mask	255.255.255.0
DNS server	192.128.32.01
Gateway	192.128.32.10
Name of registered domain	southernbell.com

Learning Objectives

In this lab, you'll install DNS on a root server and configure it with its first zone. By the end of this lab, you'll be able to:

- Install DNS
- Create a root server
- Create and configure a DNS zone

Lab Materials and Setup

This lab will require the following items:

- A working computer
- Installed network card
- Windows 2000 Server software

lab
(h)int *You should also have a Windows 2000 Server CD handy if you need to extract files not found on the hard drive. Also, it is recommended that prior to DNS installation, the server have a static IP address, subnet mask, and gateway (optional).*

Getting Down to Business

To install Domain Naming Service (DNS) and create your first DNS zone, you'll need to complete the following steps.

Step 1. To start the installation process, go to Networking Services.

Step 2. When the wizard is finished click OK to complete the installation.

lab
Hint *Now that you've installed DNS, your next task is to configure a zone for the name server.*

Step 3. Launch DNS Console.

Step 4. Configure the server as the first DNS server on the network.

Step 5. Create a standard primary forward lookup zone.

Step 6. Enter the domain name.

Step 7. Follow the wizard steps to create a reverse lookup zone. Finish the process.

LAB EXERCISE 2.02

Configuring a Standard Primary Forward and Reverse Lookup Zone

10 Minutes

In part one of this case study, you utilized the DNS initial configuration wizard to establish the standard primary and reverse lookup zones for southernbell.com.

In part two of this case study, you'll proceed with the configuration of the DNS server by creating a second standard primary forward lookup zone and a reverse lookup zone for the hr subdomain of southernbell.com. The information you need to configure the server is:

Name of primary zone	hr.southernbell.com
IP address of reverse lookup zone	192.128.32

Learning Objectives

The forward lookup zone resolves the domain's name, returns the IP address associated with it, and connects you with the web site. The reverse lookup zone does the opposite; it resolves an IP address with the domain name associated with the number. By the end of this lab, you will know how to:

■ Create a standard primary forward lookup zone

■ Create a reverse lookup zone

Lab Material and Setup

This lab will require the following:

■ A working computer

■ Installed network card

■ Windows 2000 Server software

Getting Down to Business

To begin configuring the Primary forward lookup zone and reverse lookup zone:

Step 1. Launch DNS Console.

Step 2. Choose New Zone Wizard.

Step 3. Follow the wizard to configure a standard primary forward zone.

Step 4. Create a new DNS file.

Step 5. Make sure the Create reverse lookup zone is checked.

Step 6. Follow the wizard to configure a standard primary reverse lookup zone and finish the configuration process.

LAB EXERCISE 2.03

Adding Delegated Zone for DNS

10 Minutes

In part three of this case study, you'll proceed with the configuration of a delegated zone and assignment of the server within the zone that will service requests for personal payroll information from employees.

The information you need to configure the server is as follows:

Name of delegated zone	payroll
Name of server in delegated zone	numbers.southernbell.com (192.128.32.3)

Learning Objectives

In this lab exercise, you'll create a zone delegated to handle DNS queries as a secondary source. The queries designated to the existing domain will be referred to the name server in the delegated zone. By the end of this lab, you will know how to:

■ Create a delegated zone

Lab Materials and Setup

This lab will require the following:

■ A working computer

■ Installed network card

■ Windows 2000 Server software

Getting Down to Business

Step 1.   Launch DNS Console.

Step 2.   Right-click the southernbell.com domain.

Step 3.   From the context menu, select New Delegation.

Step 4.   Type in the delegated domain.

Step 5.   Select the name server which will host the delegated zone.

Step 6.   Follow the wizard to complete the process.

LAB ANALYSIS TEST

1. While creating a DNS standard primary zone, Josh, a junior network administrator, forgets to create a reverse lookup zone. List the steps he would need to take to accomplish this task.

   _____

   _____

2. Madeline, the human resource director, is questioning why you've been called in to create a second zone for her DNS server. Although she knows nothing about the process, she would like a brief explanation in layman's terms. Give your explanation below.

   _____

   _____

3. You receive a call from Josh again, with a question about the configuration requirements for a server before installing DNS. He doesn't remember what they are. Would you help him out? Write your answer to Josh below.

   _____

   _____

4. Why would you need to implement a delegated zone for DNS?

   _____

   _____

5. What functions do forward lookup zone and reverse lookup zone perform?

   _____

   _____

KEY TERM QUIZ

Use the following vocabulary terms to complete the sentences below. Not all of the terms will be used. Definitions of these terms can be found in *MCSE Windows 2000 Directory Services Study Guide* (ISBN: 0-07-212380-X).

      domain

      domain naming service (DNS)

      Dynamic Host Configuration Protocol (DHCP)

      forward lookup zone

      reverse lookup zone

      zone

      delegated zone

      record type

      hierarchy

      lease

1. A _____ is a DNS zone table, which lists host names and the corresponding IP address.

2. A _____ receives DNS queries that are referred from another server for resolution.

3. A _____ is a special DNS zone table that contains IP address pointers to the corresponding host name.

4. A hierarchical naming system used to resolve a host name with its IP address is called _____.

5. A domain for which a DNS server has authority is called a _____.

LAB WRAP-UP

In this chapter we've been introduced to the domain naming system (DNS). This system provides your network with a host server whose database associates the name of a web site with its corresponding IP address.

The labs had you perform basic installation functions; zone creation with primary lookup zone and reverse lookup zone; and create a delegated zone to help resolve web site names to their IP address within another lower domain. You've seen that the process is straightforward, with the help of the built-in wizards.

LAB SOLUTIONS FOR CHAPTER 2

In this section, you'll find solutions to the lab exercises, lab analysis test, and key term quiz.

Lab Solution 2.01

Your task is to install DNS, a component of Windows 2000, and set up a primary DNS zone for the company's headquarters building. The information you need is the server's IP address (192.128.32.01), the subnet mask (255.255.255.0) which indicates which parts of the IP address make up the domain address, the DNS server (192.128.32.01), gateway (192.128.32.10), and name of registered domain (southernbell.com).

This lab has you install DNS on a root server and configure it with its first zone. By the end of this lab, you will have performed the following:

- Install DNS
- Create a root server
- Create and configure a DNS zone

To start the installation process:

Step 1.   Launch Add/Remove programs from the control panel.

Step 2.   Select the Add/Remove Windows Components button.

Step 3.   Select Networking Services from the Components Wizard dialog box.

Step 4.   Check the DNS box and click OK as shown in Figure 2-1.

Step 5.   When the wizard is finished click OK to complete the installation. Now that you've installed DNS, your next task is to configure a zone for the name server.

Step 6.   Launch DNS Console through the admin tools.

Step 7.   Right-click on the name server.

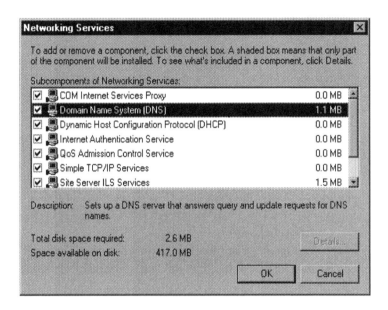

Step 8. Choose Configure the Server and click Next.

Step 9. Select Network radio button as shown in Figure 2-2.

Step 10. Select Yes, Create a forward lookup zone and click Next.

Step 11. Select Choose Standard Primary.

Step 12. Click Next and enter the domain name.

Step 13. Select Create a reverse lookup zone as shown in Figure 2-3.

Step 14. Follow the wizard steps to create a reverse lookup zone.

Step 15. Click Next to finish.

FIGURE 2-2

Select Network
radio button

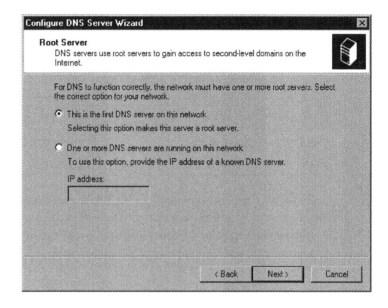

FIGURE 2-3

Select Create a
reverse lookup
zone

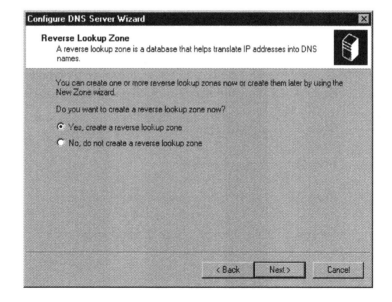

Lab Solution 2.02

In part two of this case study, this lab continues with the configuration of the DNS server by creating a second standard primary forward lookup zone and a reverse lookup zone. The information needed to configure the server is:

Company domain name	southernbell.com
Name of primary zone	hr.southernbell.com
IP address of reverse lookup zone	192.128.32

The forward lookup zone resolves the subdomain's name, hr (human resources), and returns the IP address associated with it then connects you with the web site. The reverse lookup zone does the opposite; it resolves an IP address with the domain name associated with the number. This lab has you:

- Create a standard primary forward lookup zone
- Create a reverse lookup zone

To start configuring the primary forward lookup zone and reverse lookup zone:

Step 1. Launch DNS console through the Admin Tools.

Step 2. Right-click on the name server.

Step 3. Choose New Zone Wizard and click Next.

Step 4. Follow the wizard to configure a standard primary forward zone.

Step 5. Enter the zone name, hr.southernbell.com.

Step 6. Create a new DNS file.

Step 7. Click Finish to complete the configuration.

Step 8. Make sure the Create reverse lookup zone is checked.

Step 9.   Follow the wizard to configure a standard primary reverse lookup zone as shown in Figure 2-4.

Step 10.   Once you've made the necessary entries click Finish.

Lab Solution 2.03

In the last part of this case study, you finished configuring DNS with a delegated zone and assigned a server within the zone that will service requests for personal payroll information from employees.

You were given the following information:

Name of delegated zone	payroll
Name of server in delegated zone	numbers.southernbell.com (192.128.32.3)

You have created a zone delegated to handle DNS queries as a secondary source. The queries designated to the existing domain will be referred to the name server in the delegated zone.

Follow the wizard to configure a standard primary reverse lookup zone

Step 1. Launch DNS console.

Step 2. Right-click on the zone you would like to delegate.

Step 3. From the context menu select New Delegation.

Step 4. Type in the delegated domain as shown in Figure 2-5.

Step 5. Select the name server which will host the delegated zone as shown in Figure 2-6.

Step 6. Click Finish.

ANSWERS TO LAB ANALYSIS TEST

1. Click Start | Administrative Tools | DNS. Right-click on the name server, choose New Zone Wizard, select Reverse Look Zone.

2. A DNS zone is a logical grouping of hostnames. When creating a new zone, for example hr.southerbell.com, the information for the human resources host is stored there.

FIGURE 2-5

Type in the
delegated domain

New Delegation Wizard

Delegated Domain Name
Specify the name of the domain you want to create.

Authority for the domain you create will be delegated to a different zone.

Delegated domain:
`payroll`

Fully qualified domain name:
`payroll.hr.southernbell.com`

< Back   Next >   Cancel

FIGURE 2-6

Select the name
server which will
host the
delegated zone

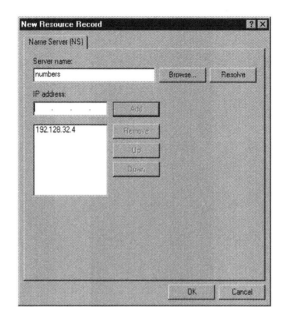

3. Prior to installing DNS, the server needs a static IP address, subnet mask, and gateway (optional).

4. A delegated zone assumes some of the responsibility for zone database management. It's a way of partitioning the database into zones that is based on certain criteria, such as geographical location and department organization.

5. The forward lookup zone holds resource records that map web site, or host names to IP addresses. The reverse lookup zone resolves IP addresses by pointing back to the web site or host name.

ANSWERS TO KEY TERM QUIZ

1. forward lookup zone

2. delegated zone

3. reverse lookup zone

4. domain naming service (DNS)

5. zone

MICROSOFT CERTIFIED SYSTEMS ENGINEER

3

Installing, Configuring, and Troubleshooting DNS

LAB EXERCISES

T he previous lab chapter worked with the basic concepts of the Domain Name Service. We installed DNS, added zones with primary forward and reverse lookup zones, and set up a delegated zone to handle some of the domain name-to-IP address resolution requests.

In this chapter we'll work with additional DNS configuration tools that help with integrating DNS with Active Directory, Dynamic Host Configuration Protocol server, and the monitoring and management of DNS using NSLOOKUP, and System Monitor. There may still be some confusion as to what DNS is all about. Let's consider that DNS is an organizational chart where each level component (domain) has additional level components (domains) below them.

LAB EXERCISE 3.01

Host Name Resolution

5 Minutes

As a support desk associate at Read-a-Lot Bookstores, you field at least 100 calls a day. Today's no different. And just when you thought you received that last call of the day, you get one from an assistant manager at your Mashpee, Mass. store. For the past two hours they have been experiencing problems resolving some web site names when assisting customers. Your first intuition leads you to verify that the DNS server is on-line. Use the NSLOOKUP utility to resolve the problem.

Learning Objectives

In this lab, you'll verify that the host name of the DNS server used to resolve domain names has an IP address associated with it. By the end of this lab, you'll be able to:

- Use NSLOOKUP
- Resolve an IP address from a host name

Lab Materials and Setup

This lab will require the following items:

■ A working computer

■ Installed network card

■ Windows 2000 Server software

Getting Down to Business

To perform a query test of a DNS server, perform the following:

Step 1. Start a DOS session.

Step 2. Use the NSLOOKUP utility to test your DNS server.

Step 3. The results verify that your DNS server is functioning.

lab
(i)int *Based on this result, some other corrective action is needed to resolve the user's name resolution issue.*

LAB EXERCISE 3.02

Setting DNS for Dynamic Updates

10 Minutes

As the junior system manager of Maxwell's Hammer and Tool Corp., you've been helping with upgrading the system to Windows 2000. You now need to make sure that the workstations register in DNS when logging in to the network. How should you configure the DNS server to make this happen?

Learning Objectives

Dynamic DNS is a combination of DHCP, DNS, and client registration working in harmony. DHCP is actually responsible for dynamic updates of both A and PTR records for down-level clients. In this lab you will:

■ Configure DNS to allow for dynamic updates

Lab Material and Setup

This lab will require the following:

■ A working computer

■ Installed network card

■ Windows 2000 Server software

Getting Down to Business

To begin configuring Dynamic DNS perform the following:

Step 1. Launch DNS console.

Step 2. Select the zone you wish to configure.

Step 3. Set the Allow Dynamic Updates option to Yes.

Step 4. Complete the process.

Integrating Windows 2000 Server with Active Directory

10 Minutes

As the system administrator of Take-a-Hike Sports Stores, you've been asked by the system's engineer to enable integration of all the store's user login, and have the computer's IP address register automatically with the company's DNS server. How would you go about configuring your DNS server to have this take place?

Learning Objectives

Active directory provides a domain-based database of objects, its properties, and values, which organizes and provides secure access to resources. In this lab exercise, you'll adjust the DNS settings to integrate with Active Directory. By the end of this lab, you will know how to:

- Integrate DNS with an Active Directory server
- Convert a standard primary zone to an active directory integrated zone

Lab Materials and Setup

This lab will require the following:

- A working computer
- Installed network card
- Windows 2000 Server software with active directory installed (dcpromo)

Getting Down to Business

To begin integrating DNS with Active Directory, perform the following:

Step 1. Launch DNS console.

Step 2. Select the Forward Lookup Zone item.

Step 3.   Select Properties from the Action menu.

Step 4.   Change the type of zone from Primary to Active Directory-Integrated.

Step 5.   Complete the process to apply your changes.

LAB EXERCISE 3.04

Integrating Windows 2000 Server with DHCP

10 Minutes

You are the operations manager of the We're-in-the-Money Investment Firm. You've just upgraded your system and the firm's 30 computers to Windows 2000. You need to configure your server to dynamically assign IP addresses to computers when they log in. How would you configure the DHCP service to work with the DNS server?

Learning Objectives

DHCP provides for the dynamic distribution and configuration of IP addresses to hosts that access the network. In this lab exercise, you'll confirm that the DHCP settings are in place to interact with the DNS server. By the end of this lab, you will know how to:

■ Configure DHCP for DNS integration

Lab Materials and Setup

This lab will require the following:

■ A working computer

■ Installed network card

■ Windows 2000 Server software

Getting Down to Business

Step 1. Launch DHCP console.

Step 2. Select the DHCP server.

Step 3. Access the Properties window of the DHCP server.

Step 4. Verify the default settings in the DNS window.

Step 5. Exit out of all windows.

LAB EXERCISE 3.05

Configuring DNS Client

5 Minutes

The second part of the previous scenario is to configure the 30 office computers to receive the dynamic IP addresses from the DHCP service. What adjustments are necessary on those computers to have this occur?

Learning Objectives

Users that access the network need to have their computer properly configured in order to interact with the DNS server. In this lab exercise, you'll configure the client computer to obtain an IP address automatically, and to register and associate that IP address with that computer in DNS. By the end of this lab, you will know how to:

■ Set automatic IP address assignment
■ Configure for IP address registration in DNS

Lab Materials and Setup

This lab will require the following:

- A working computer
- Installed network card
- Windows 2000 Professional software

Getting Down to Business

To begin the process perform the following:

Step 1. Access the Properties window of Network Neighborhood.

Step 2. Open the TCP/IP Properties window.

Step 3. Configure the properties to obtain the IP address automatically.

Step 4. Configure the properties to obtain DNS server address automatically.

Step 5. Within the Advanced TCP/IP Settings window, allow the client computer to register address in DNS.

Step 6. Click the OK button and exit out of all open windows.

LAB EXERCISE 3.06

Troubleshooting DNS Using System Monitor

20 Minutes

As you enter your office this morning, there is the following message from a client on your answering machine: "Hi Andrew, this is Josh (the distribution computer system manager) from Bright Ideas Lighting Distributors. It's 5:45 P.M. on Thursday. I didn't want to beep you since I don't see this as a critical situation. I figure it can wait until tomorrow when you get into the office. Anyway, we seem to be having a problem with the system. I've noticed that over the past two weeks the server keeps losing available memory and I've had to reboot the system at least once each week. I've actually had to reboot twice this week. I've looked at the processes running in Task Manager and noticed that the memory used by DNS.exe keeps increasing over a week's time. Once I reboot the system, all is well again until the end of the week when I have to reboot again. Would you come over sometime tomorrow and help resolve this problem? Thanks, talk to you tomorrow."

Learning Objectives

Based on the information given in the voice-mail message it seems to you that something is occurring with the DNS executable. You've given Josh a call and will be going there later this morning.

Because DNS is an important component of a network, keeping tabs of it's performance can provide a useful tool for either predicting a problem or optimizing DNS server performance. In this lab exercise we're concerned with solving a problem. So, you'll configure the System Monitor to track and interpret certain DNS counters. By the end of this lab, you will know how to:

- Configure DNS Performance Monitor
- Interpret System Monitor statistics

Lab Materials and Setup

This lab will require the following:

- A working computer
- Installed network card
- Windows 2000 Server software

Getting Down to Business

To begin the monitoring process, perform the following:

Step 1. Access the Performance utility.

Step 2. Select the System Monitor component.

Step 3. Add the following counters to track:

- Process—DNS
- Page file bytes
- Working set bytes

Step 4. Close out of Add Counters window.

Step 5. Track the counters.

Based on the results of tracking the counters and the information given to you by Josh, you determine that there's a memory leak in the DNS server. You've checked online documentation and found a resolution.

LAB ANALYSIS TEST

1. You are the computing administrator of Land Line Telephone Company. You have one DNS server resolving names for your Internet domain. You need to configure DNS on client computers to resolve Internet addresses. How would you configure them?

    _____

    _____

2. You manage the Windows 2000 DNS server for the Hithem Up Charity Organization. You need to make sure workstations are registered properly in DNS for Active Directory integration. How would configure the server?

    _____

    _____

3. You are the network administrator for Morris Clothiers. You have installed a Windows 2000 DNS server, but users are unable to resolve domain names. You need to test the server. How would you do that?

    _____

    _____

4. You are the LAN administrator of the The Santiago Church Diocese. You are running a network with six Windows 2000 DNS servers for your domain. One of the secondary servers doesn't seem to be receiving updates. How can you check to verify that the server is getting the updates?

    _____

    _____

5. What benefits do DNS clients obtain from the dynamic update feature of Windows 2000?

    _____

    _____

KEY TERM QUIZ

Use the following vocabulary terms to complete the sentences below. Not all of the terms will be used.

> NSLOOKUP
>
> Active Directory
>
> Dynamic Domain Name Service (DDNS)
>
> Domain Name Server (DNS) server
>
> dcpromo
>
> Task Manager
>
> System Monitor
>
> PTR record
>
> object
>
> zone

1. The service that stores information about objects on a network is called _____.

2. _____ is a command-line utility that allows you to make DNS queries for testing a DNS installation.

3. _____ is a process in which a workstation's name and address are entered into a table when an IP address is obtained through DHCP.

4. The service that provides dynamic name and address resolution in a TCP/IP environment is called _____.

5. A(n) _____ is an entity such as a file, folder, or Active Directory item described by a distinct, named set of attributes.

LAB WRAP-UP

In this chapter we've worked with additional key components of a Windows 2000 DNS server in a Windows 2000 environment.

In the labs, you configured additional DNS server components: set DNS for dynamic updates, integrated the server with active directory server and DHCP, and configured client computers to use DNS services. Additionally, one lab had you utilize one of the DNS server utilities (NSLOOKUP), and one lab had you add three DNS server components to monitor the performance of these counters using the Performance Console.

LAB SOLUTIONS FOR CHAPTER 3

Lab Solution 3.01

In this lab, you need to verify that the host name of the DNS server used to resolve domain names has an IP address associated with it. By the end of this lab, you are able to:

- Use NSLOOKUP

- Resolve an IP address from a host name

To perform a query test of a DNS server, perform the following:

Step 1. Start a DOS session.

Step 2. Use the NSLOOKUP utility to test your DNS server as shown in Figure 3-1.
This command is simple, fast, and straightforward. You'll notice that the command alone will elicit a response from your DNS server. You can also place either a domain name or the IP address after the command and get similar appropriate responses.

FIGURE 3-1	
Type the NSLOOKUP command in the DOS window	

```
C:\NTSRVR\System32\command.com
Microsoft(R) Windows DOS
(C)Copyright Microsoft Corp 1990-1999.

C:\>nslookup
Default Server:   benefits.southernbell.com
Address:   192.128.32.1

>
```

Lab Solution 3.02

Dynamic DNS is a combination of DHCP, DNS, and client registration working in harmony. DHCP is actually responsible for dynamic updates. In this lab you need to have workstations register with DNS when logging into the network. By the end of this lab you are able to:

- Configure DNS to allow for dynamic updates
- Configure the DHCP server to automatically update DNS changes

To begin configuring Dynamic DNS perform the following:

Step 1. Click Start | Programs | Administrative Tools.

Step 2. Launch DNS console.

Step 3. Select the zone you wish to configure.

Step 4. Right-click and select Properties.

Step 5. In the General Tab window set the Allow Dynamic Updates option to Yes as shown in Figure 3-2.

By enabling Dynamic DNS updates, the client computers will automatically register and update their information with a DNS server whenever changes occur. This reduces the administrative overhead involved with managing those DNS changes manually for each client computer.

Lab Solution 3.03

Active directory provides a domain-based database of objects, it properties, and values, which organizes and provides secure access to resources. In this lab exercise, you adjust the DNS settings to integrate with active directory. By the end of this lab, you are able to:

- Integrate DNS with an active directory server
- Convert a standard primary zone to an active directory integrated zone

FIGURE 3-2

Select Yes from
the pull down
menu

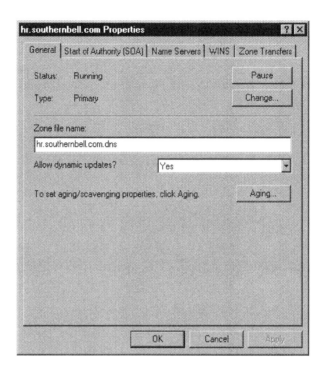

To begin the integration process, perform the following:

Step 1.   Click Start | Programs | Administrative Tools.

Step 2.   Launch DNS console.

Step 3.   In the console tree select the Zones folder.

Step 4.   Select the Forward Lookup Zone item.

Step 5.   Select Properties from the Action menu.

Step 6.   Change the type of zone from Primary to Active Directory-Integrated as shown in Figure 3-3.

Step 7.   Click the OK button to apply your changes.

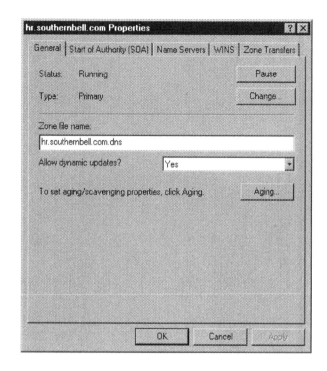

FIGURE 3-3

Select the Change button to access the zone options screen

Lab Solution 3.04

DHCP provides for the dynamic distribution and configuration of IP addresses to hosts that access the network. In this lab exercise, you confirm that the DHCP settings are in place to interact with the DNS server. By the end of this lab, you know how to:

■ Configure DHCP for DNS integration

To begin the configuration process, perform the following:

Step 1. Click Start | Programs | Administrative Tools.

Step 2. Launch DHCP console.

Step 3. Select the DHCP server.

Step 4 Access the Properties window of the DHCP server as shown in Figure 3-4.

FIGURE 3-4

Verify the settings
in this window

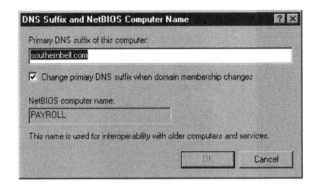

Step 5. Verify the default settings in the DNS window.

Step 6. Exit out of all windows.

The steps to configure the DHCP server to automatically update DNS changes really involve steps to verify that the default settings are in place. The DNS properties screen has several items that are checked off. You need to be sure that by default those items shown in Figure 3-4 above are the ones that have been made active. The default DHCP DDNS settings will work with Win2K clients; the last option that enables registration of both the A and PTR records must be enabled for downlevel clients. These settings will ensure that the DHCP server will update any DNS server configured as part of the server's TCP/IP network properties. The DHCP server queries its preferred DNS server for the State of Authority (SOA) for the domain and will use the Primary DNS from the SOA to register dynamic updates.

Lab Solution 3.05

Users that access the network need to have their computer properly configured in order to interact with the DNS server. In this lab exercise, you needed to configure the client computer to obtain an IP address automatically and to register and associate each IP address with each computer in DNS. By the end of this lab, you know how to:

■ Set automatic IP address assignment
■ Configure for IP address registration in DNS

To begin the configuration process, perform the following:

Step 1. Access the Properties window of Network Neighborhood.

Step 2. Open the TCP/IP Properties window.

Step 3. Configure the properties to obtain the IP address automatically.

Step 4. Configure the properties to obtain DNS server address automatically as shown in Figure 3-5.

Step 5. Within the Advanced TCP/IP Settings window, allow the client computer to register address in DNS.

Step 6. Click the OK button and exit out of all open windows.

FIGURE 3-5

Check the radio buttons to obtain IP & DNS server addresses automatically

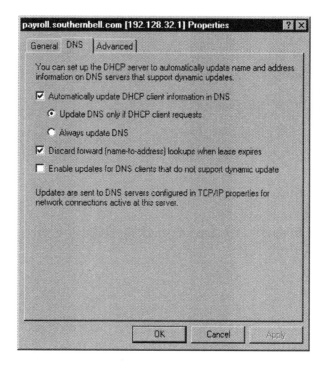

Lab Solution 3.06

Because DNS is an important component of a network, keeping tabs of its performance can provide a useful tool for either predicting a problem or optimizing DNS server performance. In this lab exercise we're concerned with solving a problem. So, you configured the System Monitor to track and interpret certain DNS counters, Process-DNS, Page file bytes, and Working set bytes. By the end of this lab, you know how to:

- Configure DNS Performance Monitor
- Interpret System Monitor statistics

To begin the monitoring process, perform the following:

Step 1. Click Start | Programs | Administrative Tools.

Step 2. Access the Performance Monitor utility.

Step 3. Select the System Monitor component on the left side of the window as shown in Figure 3-6.

Step 4. Add the following counters to track as shown in Figure 3-7.

- Process—DNS
- Page file bytes
- Working set bytes

Step 5. Close the Add Counters window.

Step 6. You can now track the selected counters as shown in Figure 3-8.

FIGURE 3-6

Click the + symbol
in the right
window to access
the Add Counters
window

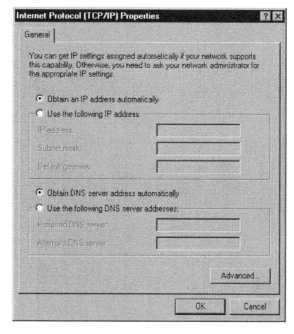

FIGURE 3-7

Select the
counters from the
Add Counters
window

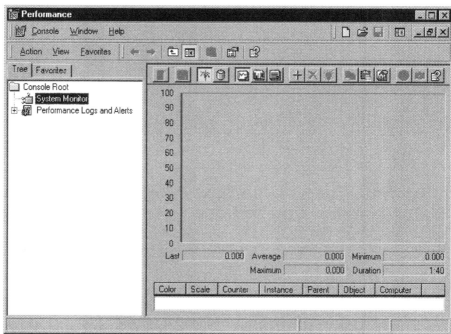

The selected
counters are
represented in
graph form

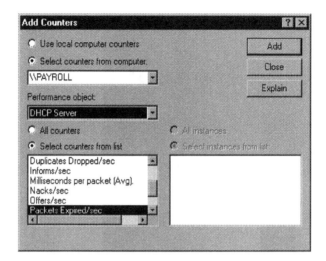

ANSWERS TO LAB ANALYSIS TEST

1. Configure the DNS settings on each client computer. You will need to access the TCP/IP protocol properties to resolve to the DNS server. The server will automatically forward any request to the appropriate server.

2. You need to configure the appropriate zone to accept dynamic updates. To accept dynamic updates, each zone needs to be configured individually.

3. Either open a DOS session, or open the RUN window. Then type NSLOOKUP along with the address of the DNS server. This will verify whether the server is configured properly.

4. Open Performance Console and click the Add Counter icon on the tool bar. Select the DNS Server object and then select the Zone Transfer Success counter. Track this counter to confirm that the secondary server is getting the updates.

5. The dynamic update feature allows DNS client computers to automatically register and update their login information with a DNS server whenever changes happen. This reduces the overhead of manually making those changes.

ANSWERS TO KEY TERM QUIZ

1. Active Directory
2. NSLOOKUP
3. DDNS
4. DNS
5. Object

MICROSOFT CERTIFIED SYSTEMS ENGINEER

4

Installing, Configuring, and Troubleshooting Dynamic Host Configuration Protocol

LAB EXERCISES

Dynamic Host Configuration Protocol (DHCP) is one of the top ten inventions of the Internet community. Why? Because it provides a vehicle to randomly assign an IP address to a user's computer without the user's intervention. This has become very useful to you and your ISP provider. It also has become very handy for you as a network manager. Without it, any change to a computer's IP address would have to be changed anytime the computer changed subnets or, you had to rearrange your IP address strategy. Because each computer's IP address is set as static, you or the user would have to physically go into the TCP/IP network properties and change the address. If this involves one, maybe two, machines once in a blue moon, no big deal. In a large-scale environment it would be a major undertaking. As an extreme analogy, let's say that when you get your driver's license, the number for that state is etched on the windshield of your car. Now, you move to another state, your license number is no longer valid in the new state. You need another license number that conforms to that state's system. Replacing the license ID is easy, but now you have to take your car in to the department of motor vehicles center and have the old number etched-out and the new one etched-in.

In this chapter we'll work with Dynamic Host Configuration Protocol (DHCP), from installing the service to configuring a DHCP scope. We'll setup a relay agent, a small program that relays DHCP/Bootstrap Protocol (BOOTP) messages between a client and a server on different subnets. We'll also work with integrating DHCP with routing and remote access service (RRAS) and Automatic Private Internet Protocol Addressing (APIPA). Lastly, we'll look at the monitoring and troubleshooting tools for DHCP.

cross
Reference

For more information refer to the section on DHCP/BOOTP in Chapter 4 of the **Windows 2000 Network Administration Study Guide.**

LAB EXERCISE 4.01

10 Minutes

Installing Dynamic Host Configuration Protocol (DHCP)

The Bay County Sheriff's Department relies on you to ensure that they are able to connect to the database on the network while on patrol. As the department has grown, the system has kept pace. Today your job is to proceed with phase one of configuring a DHCP server that will dynamically assign IP addresses to the sheriffs, installing the service on a server.

Learning Objectives

In this lab, you'll perform a basic install of DHCP services using the Configure Your Server application. By the end of this lab, you will be able to:

- Install DHCP
- Authorize a DHCP Server

Lab Materials and Setup

This lab will require the following items:

- A working computer
- Installed network card
- Windows 2000 Server software

Getting Down to Business

To begin the installation, perform the following:

Step 1. Open the Configure Your Server application.

Step 2. Follow the wizard to install DHCP.

Step 3. Confirm that DHCP is selected in the Networking Services window.

Step 4. Complete the installation.

Step 5. Launch the DHCP Manager.

Step 6. Select the DHCP server and authorize it to participate in the Active Directory.

Step 7. Complete the process.

LAB EXERCISE 4.02

Configuring Dynamic Host Configuration Protocol (DHCP) Server

10 Minutes

In the second part of the installation process at the Bay County Sheriff's Department, you now need to configure a scope, or pool, of dynamically assigned IP addresses. There are 75 sheriffs working three shifts, each shift sharing 25 squad cars with computers, plus six administration people on each shift. You need to enter the following information during configuration:

- DHCP scope name: DHCP SCOPE
- IP address range: 192.128.32.5 – 192.128.32.200
- Excluded IP address range: 192.128.32.40
- Lease duration time: 21 days
- Subnet mask: 255.255.255.0

Learning Objectives

Once DHCP is installed you need to make available a range of IP addresses that can be dynamically assigned to a host on a given subnet. This range of IP addresses is called a scope. A scope may also include values that provide configuration parameters to the client computer. In this lab you will configure a scope for your DHCP server. By the end of this lab, you will know how to:

- Create a DHCP scope
- Name a DHCP scope
- Enter a range of IP addresses
- Set the lease duration on the IP addresses
- Assign the subnet mask for the IP addresses
- Activate the scope

For more information refer to the section on Scopes in Chapter 4 of the **Windows 2000 Network Administration Study Guide**.

Lab Material and Setup

This lab will require the following:

- A working computer
- Installed network card
- Windows 2000 Server software

Getting Down to Business

To begin configuring DHCP perform the following:

Step 1. Open the DHCP Manager.

Step 2. Select the DHCP server.

Step 3. Right-click on the DHCP server and select New.

Step 4. Begin the Create Scope Wizard.

Step 5. Enter the information provided in section Configuring DHCP Server on page 4.

Step 6. In the Add Exclusions window enter excluded range of IP addresses.

Step 7. In the Lease Duration window enter a lease time.

Step 8. Complete the process by activating the scope. Options for DHCP will be configured later.

LAB EXERCISE 4.03

Configuring DCHP Relay Agents in a Routed Environment

10 Minutes

The Greenwood City School System has performed several system upgrades during the summer vacation break. The system, which resides in the administration building, has been divided into a second segment. This second segment is for access by the administrative assistants at each of the schools. In turn, this second segment needs to communicate with the school's database that resides on the first segment. To accomplish this, you need to configure a DHCP Relay Agent.

Learning Objectives

DHCP Relay Agents provide for communication between segments on a network. The Relay Agent acts as a proxy for a message traveling through routers. In this lab exercise, you'll access the RRAS monitor, then configure and activate the DHCP Relay Agent to provide for communication between segments. By the end of this lab, you will know how to:

■ Add the DHCP Relay Agent to your routing and remote access server

■ Configure your DHCP Relay Agent

lab

Warning *Routing and Remote Access Services needs to be installed before you can configure the DHCP Relay Agent. Refer to either the* **Windows 2000 Network Administration Study Guide** *or this lab manual for installation information.*

Lab Materials and Setup

This lab will require the following:

■ A working computer

■ Installed network card

■ Windows 2000 Server software

Getting Down to Business

To configure DCHP Relay Agents in a routed environment:

Step 1. Launch the Routing and Remote Access management console.

Step 2. Select General from the console tree.

Step 3. Activate the DHCP Relay Agent in the Select Routing Protocol dialog box. If you have different subnets on your network, the relay agent will allow DHCP messages between the DHCP clients and servers on those subnets.

Step 4. Click OK to complete the process.

Step 5. Right-click on the DHCP Relay Agent.

Step 6. Enter the IP address of the DHCP server.

Step 7. Click OK to complete the process.

LAB EXERCISE 4.04

5 Minutes

Integrating DCHP with Routing and Remote Access Service (RRAS)

The state's Feel Better Visiting Nurses Association has 15 nurses that service post-hospitalization patients in the state. Because the nurses work from their homes, they need to log in to the network in the morning and retrieve their assignments for the day.

Learning Objectives

The nurses connecting to your network remotely will need to have their IP addresses dynamically assigned. The close-knit relationship that exists between DHCP and RRAS allows this process to occur. In this lab exercise, you'll enable dynamic IP address assignments on the RRAS server. By the end of this lab, you will know how to:

- Configure DHCP for Remote Access

Lab Materials and Setup

This lab will require the following:

- A working computer
- Installed network card
- Windows 2000 Server software

Getting Down to Business

To integrate DCHP with Routing and Remote Access Service (RRAS):

Step 1.   Launch the Routing and Remote Access management console.

Step 2.   From the properties screen of the RRAS server, click the IP tab.

Step 3.   From here you need to ensure that IP addresses are assigned dynamically.

Step 4.   Click OK to complete the process.

LAB EXERCISE 4.05

Monitoring and Troubleshooting DHCP

10 Minutes

As administrator of the state's Get Rich Quick Lottery Commission, your days are always busy. Getting to work early sometimes has its advantages. Today, it's a different story. As the remote lottery agents are logging in to the system, you start getting complaints that the agents are getting address conflict messages when they turn on their computers. What DHCP counter might help you identify the issue?

Learning Objectives

Because DHCP is another important component of a network, keeping tabs of its performance can provide a useful tool for either predicting a problem or optimizing DHCP server performance. In this lab exercise, we're concerned with solving an IP address conflict problem. You'll configure the System Monitor to track and interpret a particular DHCP counter. By the end of this lab, you will know how to:

■ Configure DHCP performance monitor

■ Interpret System Monitor statistics

Lab Materials and Setup

This lab will require the following:

■ A working computer

■ Installed network card

■ Windows 2000 Server software

Getting Down to Business

Once DHCP is installed and configured, you may have to monitor and troubleshoot it.

Step 1. Access the Performance Monitor utility.

Step 2.   Select the System Monitor component.

Step 3.   Select the DHCP Performance object in the Add Counters window.

Step 4.   Add Declines/sec to DHCP counters to track.

Step 5.   Close the Add Counters window.

Step 6.   Track the counters.

LAB ANALYSIS TEST

1. You are the systems administrator of the new Lechmere Department Store in South Bend, Indiana. You're responsible for configuring the DHCP server added to the network that services your store. The address of the router port is 10.12.25.1, and is subnetted with a Class C subnet mask. You have 40 IP addresses you need to provide, starting with 10.12.25.20. What steps must you take to configure the server?

_____

_____

2. You are the Windows 2000 administrator for Clipped Wings Travel Agency. When checking on your DHCP server, you notice that DHCP requests are much higher than the number of users on the network. Where is the first place to look to help troubleshoot this situation?

_____

_____

3. As a consultant for Network Integration Consultants (NIC), you have been called to configure DHCP for a client. The customer is not familiar with DHCP and wants to know what information is provided to the DHCP server.

_____

_____

4. You are the network administrator for the Independent Man Insurance Company. You have a Windows 2000 Routing and Remote Access server integrated with DHCP acting as a dial-in server. You have 15 modems on the server for the insurance agents to dial-in on. Ten users have connected and are able to connect. The eleventh user is able to connect but cannot seem to reach anything on the network. What may be the problem?

_____

_____

5. The Warwick Gas Company has a network segment for its sales agents. The Windows 2000 DHCP server issues a block of 40 addresses to 120 of these sales agents. Because these agents are in and out of the office, no more than 40 of them are on the network at one particular time. What needs to be done to the DHCP server to ensure that users get an IP address each time they log in?

_____

_____

KEY TERM QUIZ

Use the following vocabulary terms to complete the sentences below. Not all of the terms will be used.

Dynamic Host Configuration Protocol (DHCP)

Routing Protocol

Routing and Remote Access Service (RRAS)

lease

proxy

Relay Agent

scope

Virtual Private Network (VPN)

Automatic Private Internet Protocol Addressing (APIPA)

Bootstrap Protocol

1. A(n)_____ is the length of time that a client computer can use a dynamically assigned IP address.

2. The service that allows you to remotely connect to a server through dial-up or VPN is called _____.

3. The industry accepted method of automatically assigning and configuring IP addresses is called _____.

4. Available IP addresses are configured in a _____ for dynamic assignment by the DHCP server to client computers.

5. A(n) _____ is way of providing a secure, private communication between a remote client computer and your network using a public network such as the Internet.

LAB WRAP-UP

In this chapter we've worked with DHCP and its associated components within a Windows 2000 environment.

The labs had you install DHCP services, configure a scope or pool of available IP addresses to assign, setup a Relay Agent to allow client computers in one network segment to send a message to another network segment connected by a router. You configured and integrated DHCP with RRAS. Lastly, you added counters in Performance Monitor to track and help troubleshoot DHCP information.

LAB SOLUTIONS FOR CHAPTER 4

Lab Solution 4.01

In this lab, you performed a basic install of DHCP services using the Configure Your Server application. By the end of this lab, you were able to:

■ Install DHCP

■ Authorize a DHCP Server

To begin the installation, perform the following:

Step 1. Access Administrative Tools from the Start button.

Step 2. Launch the Configure Your Server application.

Step 3. From the window, choose Networking as shown in Figure 4-1.

Step 4. Select DHCP.

FIGURE 4-1

From the side menu, expand Networking

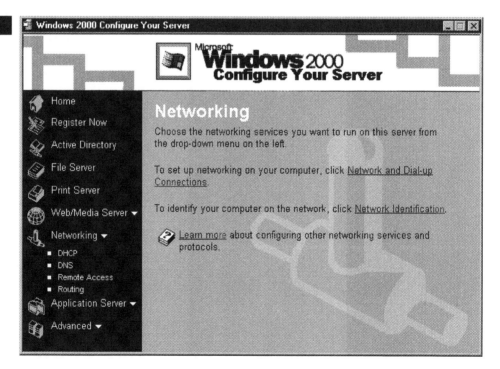

Step 5.   Click Start the Windows Components Wizard.

Step 6.   Select Networking Services in the Windows Components Wizard.

Step 7.   Click Details to see the list of Networking Services.

Step 8.   Check the box next to Dynamic Host Configuration Protocol (DHCP).

Step 9.   Click OK to complete the DHCP installation.
Now that DHCP has been installed, you need to authorize it. A DHCP server cannot assign IP addresses unless it is associated with Active Directory to be the authority in assigning IP address.

Step 10.   Launch the DHCP Manager

Step 11.   Select the DHCP server and authorize it to participate in the Active Directory, as shown in Figure 4-2.

FIGURE 4-2

From the Action menu, select Authorize

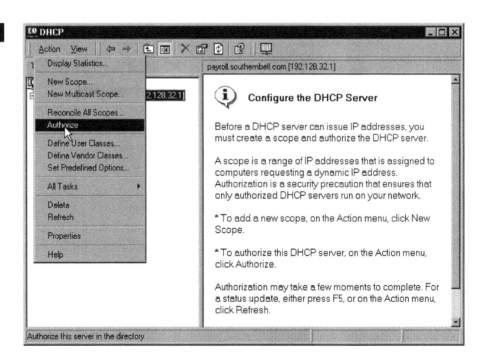

Step 12.   Complete the process.

Once finished, the scope appears with an Active status. This may take a few minutes depending on your Active Directory infrastructure.

Lab Solution 4.02

Once DHCP is installed you needed to make available a range of IP addresses that could be dynamically assigned to a host on a given subnet. This range of IP addresses is called a scope. A scope may also include values that provide configuration parameters to the client computer. You need to enter the following information during configuration:

- DHCP scope name: DHCP SCOPE
- IP address range: 192.128.32.5 – 192.128.32.200
- Excluded IP address: 192.128.32.40
- Lease duration time: 21 days
- Subnet mask: 255.255.255.0
- Parent domain:

In this lab you configured a scope for your DHCP server. By the end of this lab, you were able to:

- Create a DHCP scope
- Name a DHCP scope
- Enter a range of IP addresses
- Set the lease duration on the IP addresses
- Assign the subnet mask for the IP addresses
- Activate the scope

To begin configuring DHCP perform the following:

Step 1.   Open the DHCP Manager.

Step 2.   Select the DHCP server.

Step 3. Right-click on the DHCP server and select New.

Step 4. Begin the Create Scope Wizard.

Step 5. Enter the information provided on page 5 as shown in Figure 4-3. A DHCP scope name is necessary; a description is not.

Step 6. In the Add Exclusions window, enter the excluded range of IP addresses, as shown in Figure 4-4.

Step 7. In the Lease Duration window enter a lease time. The length of the lease is up to your discretion. Typically it depends on the design of your infrastructure, but here we provided the students 21 days as a criteria.

Step 8. Options for DHCP will be configured later.

Step 9. Select No, I Will Configure These Options Later.

FIGURE 4-3

Your start and end IP addresses are entered here

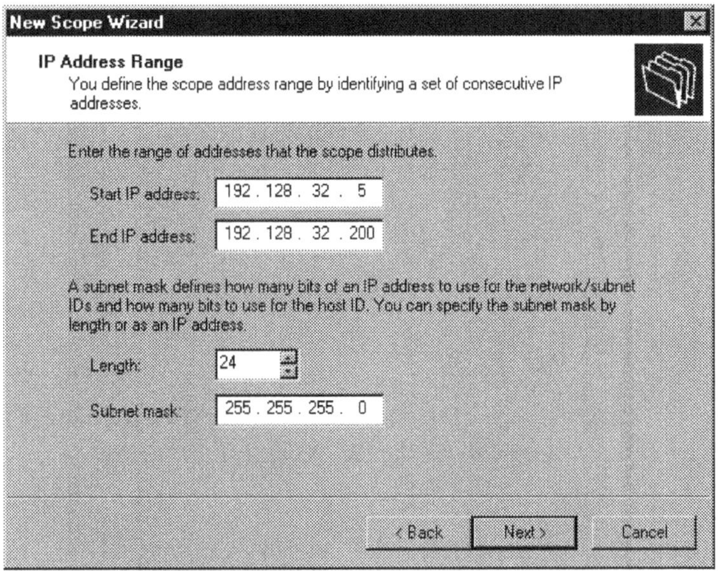

Specific IP
addresses need
to be added
individually

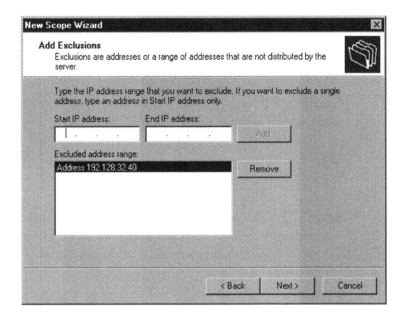

Step 10. Complete the process by activating the scope at this time.

Step 11. Select Yes, I Want To Activate The Scope Now.

Lab Solution 4.03

DHCP relay agents provide for communication between segments on a network. The Relay Agent acts as a proxy for a message traveling through routers. In this lab exercise, you accessed the RRAS monitor, configured and activated the DHCP relay agent to provide for communication between segments. By the end of this lab, you were able to:

■ Add the DHCP Relay Agent to your routing and remote access server

■ Configure your DHCP Relay Agent

lab
ⓗint
Remember that routing and Remote Access Services need to be installed before you can configure the DHCP Relay Agent.

To begin configuring DHCP perform the following:

Step 1. Access Administrative Tools from the Start button.

Step 2. Launch the Routing and Remote Access management console.

Step 3. Expand the console tree.

Step 4. Select General.

Step 5. Right-click and select New Routing Protocol.

Step 6. Activate the DHCP Relay Agent in the Select Routing Protocol dialog box. If you have different subnets on your network, the relay agent will allow DHCP messages between the DHCP clients and servers on those subnets, as shown in Figure 4-5.

FIGURE 4-5

The DHCP relay agent will appear once added

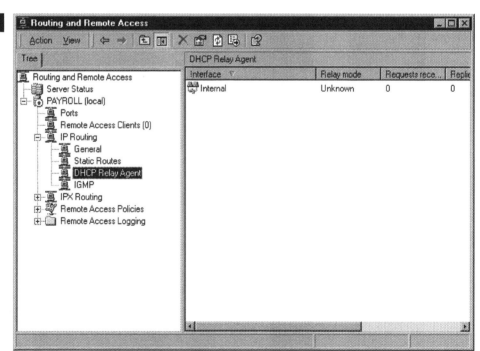

Step 7.   Click OK to complete the process.

Step 8.   Right-click on DHCP Relay Agent and select Properties.

Step 9.   Enter the IP address of the DHCP server, as shown in Figure 4-6.

Step 10.   Click OK to complete the process.

Lab Solution 4.04

The nurses connecting to your network remotely needed to have their IP addresses dynamically assigned. The close-knit relationship that exists between DHCP and RRAS allows this process to occur. In this lab exercise, you needed to enable dynamic IP address assignments on the RRAS server. By the end of this lab, you were able to:

■ Configure DHCP for remote access

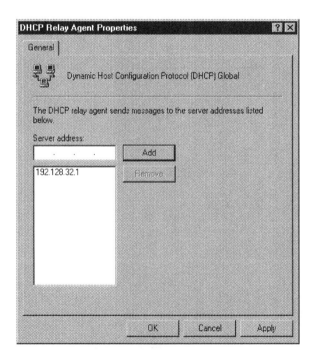

FIGURE 4-6

Your DHCP IP address is entered as a global parameter

To begin configuring DHCP perform the following:

Step 1. Access Administrative Tools from the Start button.

Step 2. Launch the Routing and Remote Access management console.

Step 3. Select the RRAS server and right-click to select Properties.

Step 4. From the Properties screen click the IP tab.

Step 5. From here you need to ensure that IP addresses are assigned dynamically. To do so you need to click Dynamic Host Configuration Protocol as shown in Figure 4-7.

Step 6. Click OK to complete the process. From this point on, the routing and remote access service (RRAS) will dynamically issue IP addresses for users.

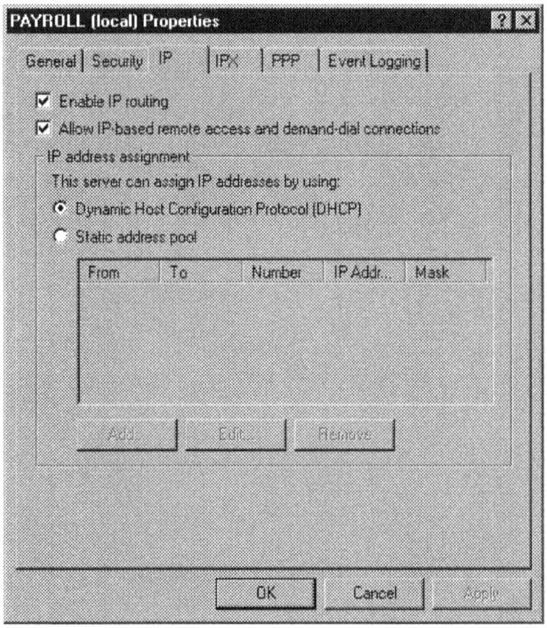

FIGURE 4-7

Configure RRAS to use DHCP to assign IP addresses

Lab Solution 4.05

Because DHCP is another important component of a network, keeping tabs of its performance can provide a useful tool for either predicting a problem or optimizing DHCP server performance. In this lab exercise we were concerned with solving an IP address conflict problem. So, you configured the System Monitor to track and interpret a particular DHCP counter. By the end of this lab, you were able to:

- Configure DHCP Performance Monitor
- Interpret System Monitor statistics

To begin configuring DHCP perform the following:

Step 1. Access the Administrative Tools from the Start button.

Step 2. Launch the Performance Monitor utility.

Step 3. Highlight the System Monitor component.

Step 4. Select the DHCP Performance object in the Add Counters window.

Step 5. Add Declines/sec to the DHCP counters to track, as shown in Figure 4-8.

Tracking the number of IP addresses that were rejected from the client computers can be an indication of either network issues, computers that have static addresses that are part of the scope, or possibly a "rogue" DHCP server on the network.

Step 6. Close the Add Counters window.

Step 7. Track the counter.

FIGURE 4-8

Select the DHCP
Server in
Performance
Object

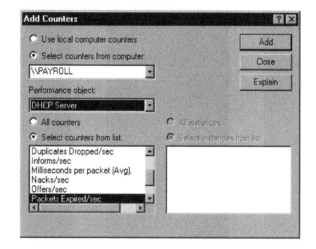

ANSWERS TO LAB ANALYSIS TEST

1. A lone DHCP server can accommodate multiple network segments, so an additional server is not needed. To get the 40 addresses, the range must be between 10.12.25.20 and 10.12.25.39, since it is an inclusive range. The last step of the Scope Wizard authorizes the new scope.

2. You may want to check the length of the DHCP lease. If the lease is set to a very short duration, client computers would need to request IP addresses frequently.

3. The information provided to the DHCP server is the client's Mac address, it's host name, and Net BIOS name by default.

4. The routing and remote access service (RRAS) requests 10 addresses from the DHCP server when it is initialized. When these ten IP addresses have been issued, RRAS will request an additional ten IP addresses. If the DHCP server has gone off-line since the original addresses were issued, the client would connect but be unable to get on the network because RRAS could not obtain the additional addresses from the DHCP server.

5. To ensure that the addresses are available, the DHCP lease duration needs to be set to a short interval.

ANSWERS TO KEY TERM QUIZ

1. lease

2. RRAS

3. DHCP

4. scope

5. VPN

5

Configuring, Managing, Monitoring, and Troubleshooting Remote Access

R emote access in Windows 2000 is achieved through a service named Routing and Remote Access Service (RRAS). Running on a Windows 2000 Server, this service allows other servers or client computers not connected to the network via a permanent cable to connect by way of phone lines, Integrated Services Digital Network (ISDN) lines, Digital Subscriber Lines (DSL), and cable modems. Once connected, the computer can access the resources on the RRAS server and other computers on the same network as the server.

In this chapter we'll work with Routing and Remote Access Service (RRAS), from installing the service to configuring connections using Point-to-Point Protocol (PPP) Multilink and Bandwidth Allocation Protocol (BAP). We'll assign remote access permissions, a set of actions that can be applied to a group of users that meet a specified set of requirements. We'll also configure a Virtual Private Network (VPN) and establish security parameters for remote access. Lastly, we'll look at the monitoring and troubleshooting tools for Routing and Remote Access Service (RRAS).

LAB EXERCISE 5.01

Installing and Configuring Remote Access   20 Minutes

The Oasis Beverage Company has grown over the past few years. In doing so their network has also grown. They've gone from one server hosting a relational database to a Windows 2000 domain server, an application server, and a database server. Due to the increased number of sales representatives you need to install a Routing and Remote Access service to the domain server. You've already added a bank of modems to the domain server, and now you need to install the Routing and Remote Access Server and configure the server for inbound connections.

Learning Objectives

Since RRAS is integrated with Windows 2000, it is present after the initial build. At this point you need to install the service for the server itself. This includes establishing the server as a router, as well as configuring an authentication and encryption method and access rights for those systems that connect.

In this lab, you'll install and configure a RRAS. By the end of this lab, you will know how to:

■ Install RRAS

■ Specify an authentication and encryption policy

■ Define access rights for remote systems

Lab Materials and Setup

This lab will require the following items:

■ A working computer

■ Installed network card

■ Installed modem

■ Windows 2000 Server software

Getting Down to Business

To begin the installation, perform the following:

Step 1.   Access the Routing and Remote Access management console.

Step 2.   Right-click the server for which you want to install remote access.

Step 3.   Click Configure and Enable Routing and Remote Access.

Step 4.   Complete the installation with the following settings:

■ Enable server as a router and local routing only

■ IPX and TCP/IP for remote client protocols

■ Designate Automatic IP Assignment

Step 5.   Verify that you have denied the use of Remote Authentication Dial-in User Service (RADIUS) on the server in the Managing Remote Access Servers window.

Step 6. Complete the process.

Now that you've installed RRAS, you want to configure Inbound Connections.

Step 7. Access the Network and Dial-up Connections window.

Step 8. Start the New Connection Wizard.

Step 9. Follow the prompts to enter the Location Information:
- Country/Region – United States
- Area Code (enter your own number)
- Tone/Pulse Dialing

lab
Hint *If you've already configured your dialing location information you will not be prompted for location information.*

Step 10. In the Network Connection Wizard window select Accept Incoming Connections.

Step 11. Select Do Not Allow Virtual Private Connections.

Step 12. Select the users/groups you want to have dial-in access.

Step 13. In the Callback tab, allow the caller to set the callback number.

Step 14. All network components are selected in the Networking Components window.

Step 15. Enter a connection name for the new configuration.

Step 16. Complete the process.

LAB EXERCISE 5.02

Assigning a Remote Access Policy

10 Minutes

In part two of your task to install a Routing and Remote Access Server, you need to perform additional configurations by applying a set of parameters by which regional directors and sales representatives dialing into the network can access the resources on the network. They need the ability to check available stock and place orders.

Learning Objectives

A Remote Access Policy is a criteria to which RRAS users are compared. When they are matched to a policy, then their permissions are examined—first their account, then if account is set to Control Access Through Remote Access Policy—their Remote Access Policy is examined to see if they have permission. Finally, if they have permission, the settings of the profile associated with their policy are applied. These settings can apply to authentication, encryption, Multilink, etc… If they don't meet the criteria of any policies, they will be denied access, regardless of their account permissions, set of actions, or parameters, that are applied to remote users determining how those remote users can dial-in and access the network.

In this lab you will configure a Remote Access Policy. By the end of this lab, you will know how to:

- Select groups for remote access permissions
- Setup dial-in constraints
- IP address assignments
- Configure IP Packet Filters
- Configure Remote Access Server encryption

Lab Material and Setup

This lab will require the following:

- A working computer
- Installed network card
- Windows 2000 Server software

Getting Down to Business

To create a Remote Access Policy perform the following:

Step 1. Access the Routing and Remote Access console.

Step 2. Expand the tree and click on Remote Access Policy.

Step 3. Give the new policy a name.

Step 4. Select a Windows-Groups attribute.

Step 5. Add a group for remote access.

Step 6. In the Permissions window grant remote access permission.

Step 7. Complete the process.

LAB EXERCISE 5.03

Installing Virtual Private Networking (VPN) 10 Minutes

Tony Autostrada started his auto parts store 40 years ago in a storefront in Olneyville. Today, Autostrada Auto Parts Co. has 35 stores in 3 states in New England. As the network engineer you need to set up private connections to your parts database server for each store manager to access. Since all of the stores have Internet connections you can provide access using the existing public connection by configuring a Virtual Private Network (VPN) for them.

Learning Objectives

A Virtual Private Network (VPN) is the ability to exchange data between two computers, a client and a server, across an internetwork in a fashion that makes the user believe that that user is connected directly, securely, and privately while using a public connection such as the Internet. It is cost effective and a solution for users that travel and need to connect from various locations.

In this lab exercise, you'll configure a Virtual Private Network (VPN). By the end of this lab, you will know how to:

- Configure ports for VPN use
- Configure a port using Point-to-Point Tunneling Protocol (PPTP)
- Configure a port using Layer 2 Tunneling Protocol (L2TP) and IP Security Protocol (IPSec)

Lab Materials and Setup

This lab will require the following:

- A working computer
- Installed network card
- Windows 2000 Server software

Getting Down to Business

To configure a new VPN demand-dial connection perform the following:

Step 1. Access the Routing and Remote Access management console.

Step 2. Expand the console tree.

Step 3. Click the Ports entry under the server.

Step 4. Right-click on the Ports and select Properties.

Step 5. Configure the PPTP device as Inbound Only remote access.

Step 6. Configure the L2TP device as a Demand Dial connection.

Step 7. Complete the process to apply your configuration options.

LAB EXERCISE 5.04

Configuring Point-to-Point Protocol Multilink and Bandwidth Allocation Protocol

10 Minutes

As network administrator of Dual Image Copy Company, you are responsible for 30 service technicians that remotely connect to the network at the end of each day to submit their completed work orders, and to retrieve their work orders for the next day. Your company provides the technicians with two modem lines to transmit. Because this happens during the hours of 4 P.M. to 6 P.M. you need to ensure that each service technician has sufficient bandwidth to complete their transmissions in an appropriate amount of time. To this end, you need to activate the Multilink Point-to-Point Protocol (PPP) and Bandwidth Allocation Protocol (BAP) settings.

Learning Objectives

Multilink allows the combination of multiple physical links to the network to appear as a single logical link where data is transmitted and received. The combined connections, called bundles, provide a much greater bandwidth than a single connection. The BAP is a PPP control protocol that is used to add or remove additional links to a multilink connection. In this lab exercise, you'll enable dynamic multilink capabilities and bandwidth allocation capabilities on the RRAS server. By the end of this lab, you will know how to:

- Configure multilink connections for remote access

Lab Materials and Setup

This lab will require the following:

- A working computer
- Installed network card
- Windows 2000 Server software

Getting Down to Business

To configure a PPP multilink connection, perform the following:

Step 1.   Access the Routing and Remote Access management console.

Step 2.   Expand the console tree.

Step 3.   Right mouse click the remote access policy you want to configure.

Step 4.   In the Profiles window select the Multilink tab.

Step 5.   Select the Allow Multilink radio button and the Require BAP For Dynamic Multilink Requests check box.

Step 6.   Click the OK button to complete the process.

LAB EXERCISE 5.05

Managing and Monitoring Remote Access   5 Minutes

You are the network administrator for the Apponoug Marine Supply Co. Keeping you network healthy means tracking and monitoring counters that affect routing and remote access in the Performance Monitor utility. Which counters do you need to add to System Monitor?

Learning Objectives

When providing Routing and Remote Access Services (RRAS), it's necessary to keep an eye on the remote services provided to clients (users). The tool for managing and monitoring RRAS is, again, Performance Monitor. You want to ensure error and problem free connections to your clients (users). In this lab you will add counters within Performance Monitor to view and track. By the end of this lab, you will know how to:

■ Configure RRAS Performance Monitoring for selected counters

■ Interpret System Monitor statistics

Lab Materials and Setup

This lab will require the following:

■ A working computer

■ Installed network card

■ Windows 2000 Server software

Getting Down to Business

To configure RRAS Performance Monitoring perform the following:

Step 1. Access the Performance Monitor utility.

Step 2. Select the System Monitor component.

Step 3. Select the RAS Port Performance object in the Add Counters window.

Step 4. Add the following RAS counter for all instances to track:

■ Bytes Transmitted

■ Bytes Received

■ Frames Transmitted

Step 5. Close out of Add Counters window.

Step 6. Track the counters.

LAB EXERCISE 5.06

Remote Access Security

5 Minutes

Ionian Importing Company had you, the network administrator, install a new Windows 2000 Routing and Remote Access server. The marketing agents overseas connect to the network via a VPN. Your U.S. regional sales representatives access the network using Point-to-Point dialers. What is the most secure way to ensure that the sales representatives have secure dial-up access?

Learning Objectives

In this lab exercise we're going to look at the method of user authentication when connecting via the Remote Access Server. So, you'll configure the server to ensure a secure entry. By the end of this lab, you will know how to:

■ Configure Remote Access Security

Lab Materials and Setup

This lab will require the following:

■ A working computer
■ Installed network card
■ Windows 2000 Server software

Getting Down to Business

To configure a Remote Access Security policy perform the following:

Step 1. Access the Routing and Remote Access console.

Step 2. Right-click on the server and select Properties.

Step 3. Set Windows Authentication in the Security Tab.

Step 4. Within the Authentication Methods window, be sure that at least one of the authentication protocols is chosen.

For further information refer to the section on Authentication Protocols in Chapter 5 of the **Windows 2000 Network Administration Study Guide.**

Step 5. Complete the process.

LAB ANALYSIS TEST

1. You are the network administrator for Xpress Service Stations, a chain of gas stations and convenience stores. As part of the network, you are responsible for a Windows 2000 Routing and Remote Access server to provide remote access services as part of a Virtual Private Network (VPN). Which VPN protocols will the server support?

   _____

   _____

2. You are the system administrator for the Coast-to-Coast Insurance Agency, a company that manages a network of independent insurance agents. These agents connect to your Windows 2000 Routing and Remote Access service from all over the country, most working from home or small office. How can you minimize the users toll charges when accessing the network?

   _____

   _____

3. As a LAN administrator, everyone in your company, Millennium Marketing, knows you as the "troubleshooter." You have an end user who is trying to connect to the Routing and Remote Access server but keeps getting the message that she is not an authorized user. Betsy is able to connect to the network and login from her office across the LAN. After doing some research you find that the user ID was not authorized for remote access. How would you fix the situation?

   _____

   _____

4. You are the Windows 2000 administrator for Creepy Crawler Pest Control. Your users are all connecting to your network using 56K modems, and they are complaining about performance. You are using a RRAS server with a modem bank. Each user is running Windows 2000 Professional on their computer. Using the performance monitoring utility you determine that there are no issues with the service. The problem seems to be bandwidth limitations. What should you do?

   _____

   _____

5. You are the network administrator for Supra Tutti Consulting Services. You have installed your first Routing and Remote Access server and your users are connecting without a problem. How would you check to see how much traffic is being added to the network by additional users?

   _____

   _____

KEY TERM QUIZ

Use the following vocabulary terms to complete the sentences below. Not all of the terms will be used.

> Callback
>
> Remote Authentication Dial-in User Server (RADIUS)
>
> Multilink
>
> Authentication
>
> Bandwidth Allocation Protocol (BAP)
>
> Internet Protocol Security (IPSec)
>
> Encryption
>
> Encapsulation
>
> Firewalls
>
> Automatic Private IP Address (APIPA)

1. A capability provided in Windows 2000, _____ allows the combined use of multiple modem connections from a Window 2000 host to a dial-up network.

2. _____ is a mechanism for securing data by translating it into a secret code. This code can only be read with the correct key, which deciphers the code back to the original data.

3. The process of verifying a user's identity when connecting to a network is called _____.

4. A serial-line protocol, _____ replaces the frame types used on networks when communicating over a serial line. It defines how data is physically transmitted.

5. The standard IP-based VPN protocol that is used to provide secure communication across a public network is called _____.

LAB WRAP-UP

In this chapter we've worked with Routing and Remote Access service within a Windows 2000 environment. This service provides remote access capabilities for external users. We started with the installation and configuration of the Routing and Remote Access Server to enable inbound connections. In another lab, you configured a remote access policy—a policy that will determine the user's access capabilities. One lab had you configure a Virtual Private Network (VPN)—a way to allow user access to your network using a public network. There were labs where you set up multilink connections, monitored Routing and Remote Access service counters using Performance Monitor, and enabled authentication protocols and encryption for Remote Access Security.

LAB SOLUTIONS FOR CHAPTER 5

Lab Solution 5.01

Since RRAS is integrated with Windows 2000, it is present after the initial build. At this point, you need to install the service for the server itself. This includes establishing the server as a router, configuring an authentication and encryption method, in addition to establishing access rights for those systems that connect.

In this lab, you installed and configured a Routing and Remote Access Server (RRAS). By the end of this lab, you would know how to:

- Install RRAS
- Specify an authentication and encryption policy
- Define access rights for remote systems

To begin the installation, perform the following:

Step 1. Click Start.

Step 2. Select Administrative Tools.

Step 3. Access the Routing and Remote Access management console.

Step 4. Right-click the server for which you want to install remote access.

Step 5. Choose Configure And Enable Routing And Remote Access.

Step 6. In the wizard click Next.

Step 7. Select Remote Access Server on the Common Configuration window as shown in Figure 5-1.

Step 8. In the Remote Client Protocols window make sure that TCP/IP is listed.

Step 9. Verify that Yes, All The Required Protocols Are On This List is selected.

FIGURE 5-1

Allow remote
users to access
the network by
enabling Remote
Access Services

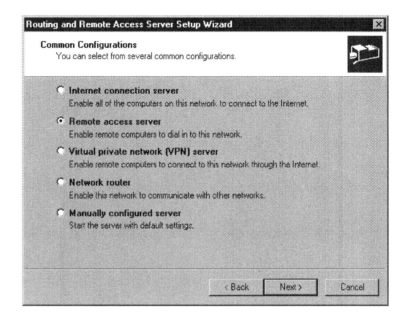

Step 10. Click Next.

Step 11. Select the IP address assignments to be automatic as shown in Figure 5-2.

Step 12. Verify that you have denied the use RADIUS on the server on the Managing Remote Access Servers window.

Step 13. Click Next .

Step 14. Click Finish to complete the process.
Now that you've installed RRAS, you want to configure an Inbound Connection.

Step 15. Access the Network and Dial-up Connections window.

Step 16. Start the New Connection Wizard.

Step 17. Follow the prompts to enter the Location Information:

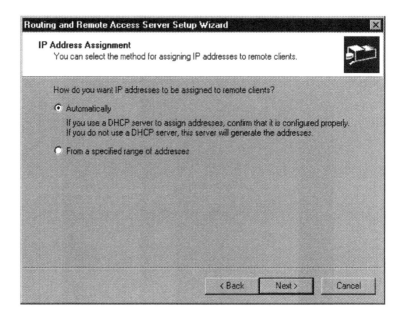

- Country/Region – United States
- Area Code (enter your own area code number)
- Tone/Pulse Dialing

lab
Hint   *If you've already configured your dialing location information you will not be
prompted for location information.*

Step 18. In the Network Connection Wizard window, select Accept Incoming
Connections as shown in Figure 5-3.

Step 19. Select Do Not Allow Virtual Private Connections.

Step 20. Select the users/groups you want to have dial-in access.

Step 21. In the callback tab allow the caller to set the callback number.

Step 22. All network components are selected in the Networking
Components window.

Select the type of connection you wish to create in the Connection Type window

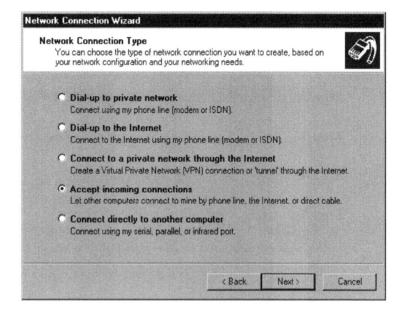

Step 23.   Enter a connection name for the new configuration (i.e. Incoming Connections).

Step 24.   Click OK to finish.

Lab Solution 5.02

A Remote Access Policy is a set of actions or parameters that are applied to remote users determining how those remote users can dial-in and access the network. In this lab you configure a remote access policy. By the end of this lab, you would know how to:

- Select groups for remote access permissions
- Setup dial-in constraints
- IP address assignments
- Configure IP Packet Filters
- Configure Remote Access Server encryption

lab
Hint   *The last three bullets above are set by default. You may adjust the settings later to meet your needs.*

To create a Remote Access Policy perform the following:

Step 1. Click Start | Programs | Administrative Tools.

Step 2. Launch the Routing and Remote Access console.

Step 3. Expand the tree and right-click on Remote Access Policy.

Step 4. Select New Remote Access Policy item.

Step 5. Give the new policy a name.

lab **Ⓗint** *In this window you need to give your policy a name, i.e. Allow Domain Users.*

Step 6. Click Next.

Step 7. Click Add to add a condition. From the list, select one of the attributes that will determine the connection parameters. Selecting Windows-Groups will allow you to enable remote access by user groups. This definition is determined in the Users and Groups console.

Step 8. Select a Windows-Groups attribute as shown in Figure 5-4.

Step 9. Click Add to go to the Groups dialog box.

Step 10. Click Add again to open the Select Groups dialog box.

Step 11. Select the Domain Users group and click Add as shown in Figure 5-5.

Step 12. Click OK to return to the Groups dialog box.

Step 13. Click Next to open the Add Remote Access Policy dialog box. In this window you have the option to grant certain access rights to a group. You can either grant access or deny access.

FIGURE 5-4

Select the criteria
by which your
remote users will
access the
network

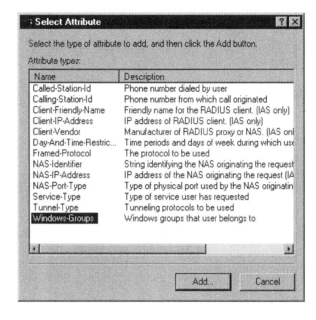

FIGURE 5-5

Add the groups
that contain
remote users

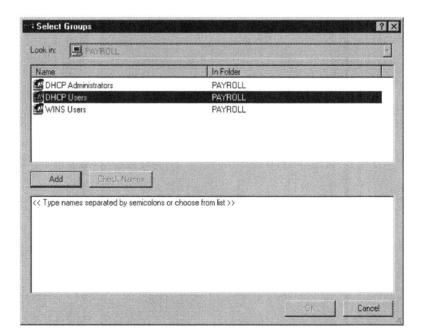

Step 14. In the Permissions window select Grant Remote Access Permission.

Step 15. Clicking Next takes you to the User Profile dialog box.

Step 16. Click Edit Profile to open the Edit Dial-in Profile window as shown in Figure 5-6. This window has several tab options which allows you to configure dial-in parameters. For this lab we leave the selections at the default settings.

Step 17. Click OK to return to the User Profile screen.

Step 18. Click Finish to complete the policy.
  The policy will be used in conjunction with the user's own dial-in settings to determine a connection is allowed. After the connection is allowed, the settings of the profile are applied.

FIGURE 5-6

Notice the six tab options to edit dial-in properties

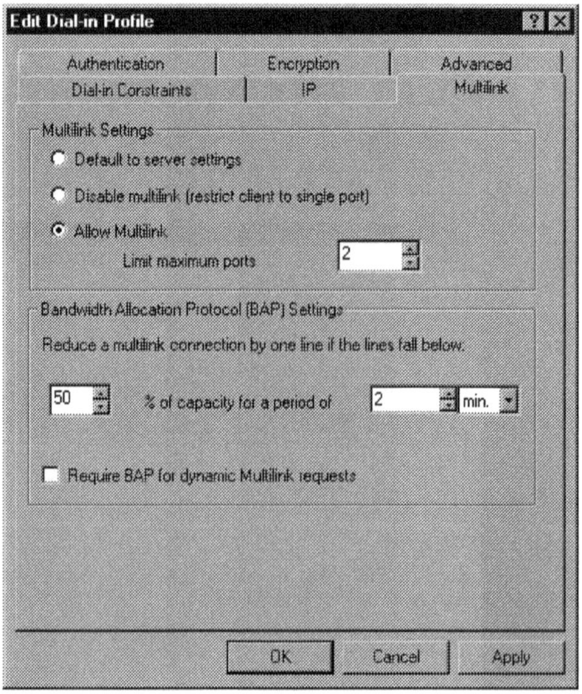

Lab Solution 5.03

A Virtual Private Network (VPN) is the ability to exchange data between two computers, a client and a server, across an internetwork in a fashion that makes the user believe that that user is connected directly, securely, and privately while using a public connection such as the Internet. It is cost effective and a solution for users that travel and need to connect from various locations.

In this lab exercise, you'll configure a Virtual Private Network (VPN). By the end of this lab, you will know how to:

- Configure ports for VPN use
- Configure a port using Point-to-Point Tunneling Protocol (PPTP)
- Configure a port using Layer 2 Tunneling Protocol (L2TP) and IP Security Protocol (IPSec)

To begin configuring ports for VPN use perform the following:

Step 1.   Click Start | Programs | Administrative Tools.

Step 2.   Access the Routing and Remote Access management console

Step 3.   Expand the console tree.

Step 4.   Right-click the Ports entry under the server as shown in Figure 5-7.

lab
Hint   *By default you will notice in the ports window, five PPTP ports and five L2TP/IPSec ports. This is due to the five-user license configured when the Routing and Remote Access Server is installed.*

Step 5.   Right-click on the Ports and select Properties.

Step 6.   The Ports Properties window opens showing a list of protocols.

Step 7.   Select the PPTP device and click Configure.

Step 8.   Configure the PPTP device as Inbound Only remote access.

FIGURE 5-7

Available ports
show on the
right pane

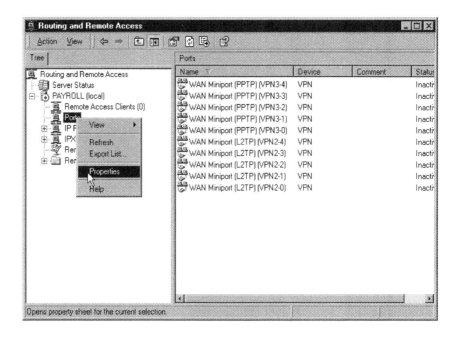

Step 9. Click OK.

Step 10. Select the L2TP device and click Configure.

Step 11. Configure the L2TP device as a Demand Dial connection.

Step 12. Click OK.

Step 13. Click OK again to complete the process and apply your configuration options.

Lab Solution 5.04

Multilink allows the combination of multiple physical links to the network to appear as a single logical link where data is transmitted and received. The combined connections, called bundles, provide a much greater bandwidth than a single connection. The Bandwidth Allocation Protocol (BAP) is a PPP control protocol that is used to add or remove additional links to a multilink connection. In this lab exercise, you'll enable dynamic multilink capabilities and bandwidth allocation capabilities on the RRAS server. By the end of this lab, you would know how to:

■ Configure Multilink connections for Remote Access

To begin configuring Multilink and BAP options perform the following:

Step 1. Click Start | Programs | Administrative Tools.

Step 2. Access the Routing and Remote Access management console.

Step 3. Expand the console tree.

Step 4. Click the Remote Access Policies to activate the right pane.

Step 5. Right-click the remote access policy you want to configure.

Step 6. Select Properties.

Step 7. Click Edit Profile.

Step 8. Select the Multilink tab.

Step 9. In the Multilink tab of the Edit Dial-in Profile window, select Allow Multilink and the Require BAP For Dynamic Multilink Requests check box as shown in Figure 5-8.

Step 10. Click OK to complete the process.

Lab Solution 5.05

When providing Routing and Remote Access Services (RRAS), it's necessary to keep an eye on the remote services provided to clients (users). The tool for managing and monitoring RRAS is, again, System Monitor.

FIGURE 5-8

Set Multilinking
and Bandwidth
Allocation

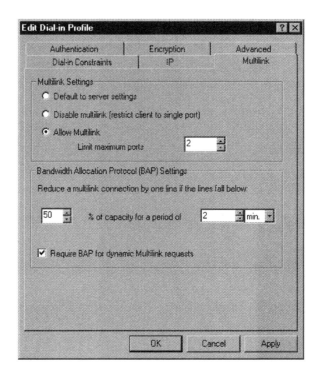

You want to ensure error- and problem-free connections to your clients (users). In this lab you added counters within Performance Monitor to view and track. By the end of this lab, you will know how to:

- Configure RRAS Performance Monitoring
- Interpret System Monitor statistics

To begin configuring, perform the following:

Step 1. Click Start | Programs | Administrative Tools.

Step 2. Launch the Performance Monitor utility.

Step 3. Select the System Monitor component.

Step 4. Click Add (+)to create an entry in System Monitor.

lab
ⒽInt

Step 5. Select RAS Port Performance in the Add Counters window.

You will notice a list of counters available for RAS displayed on the left and a list of RAS devices on the right pane.

Step 6. Add the following RAS counter for All Instances to track as shown in Figure 5-9.

- Bytes Transmitted
- Bytes Received
- Frames Transmitted

Step 7. Close out of Add Counters window.

Step 8. Track the counters.
You will now see your counters being graphed.

Lab Solution 5.06
In this lab exercise you looked at the method of configuring user authentication when connecting via the Remote Access Server. By default, the Authentication

FIGURE 5-9

Selecting counters for Remote Access tracking

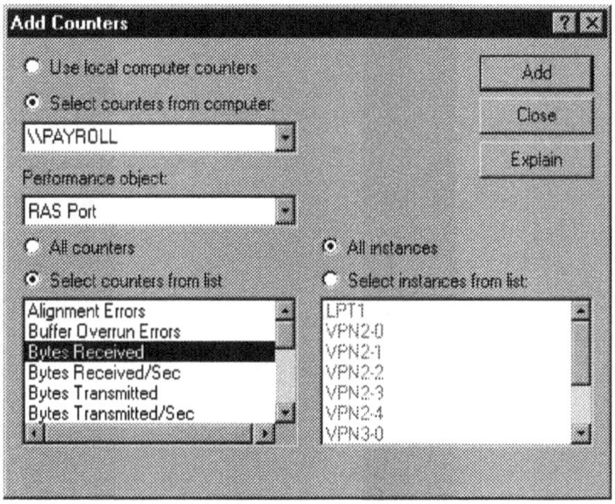

Add Counters

- ○ Use local computer counters
- ● Select counters from computer:
  \\PAYROLL

[Add]
[Close]
[Explain]

Performance object:
RAS Port

- ○ All counters
- ● Select counters from list:

- ● All instances
- ○ Select instances from list:

Alignment Errors	LPT1
Buffer Overrun Errors	VPN2-0
Bytes Received	VPN2-1
Bytes Received/Sec	VPN2-2
Bytes Transmitted	VPN2-3
Bytes Transmitted/Sec	VPN2-4
	VPN3-0

Provider is set at Windows Authentication. So, your task here is to verify that the server is set as such. By the end of this lab, you would know how to:

■ Configure Remote Access Security

To verify the Remote Access Security setting perform the following:

Step 1. Click Start | Programs | Administrative Tools.

Step 2. Launch the Routing and Remote Access console.

Step 3. Right-click on the server and select Properties.

Step 4. Select the Security tab.

Step 5. Verify that Windows Authentication is set in the Security Tab as shown in Figure 5-10.

FIGURE 5-10

Security validates remote users' credentials

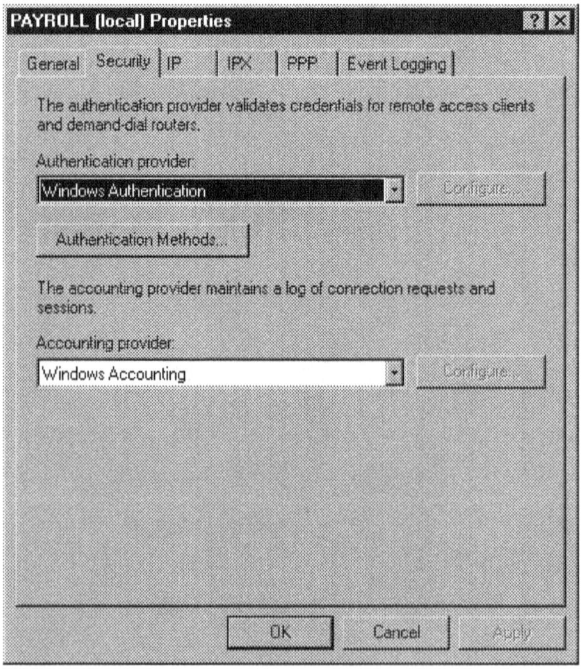

Step 6. Within the Authentication Methods window, be sure that at least one of the authentication protocols is chosen.

*For more information refer to the section on the various authentication protocols in Chapter 5 of the **Windows 2000 Network Administration Study Guide.***

Step 7. Click OK to close the window.

ANSWERS TO LAB ANALYSIS TEST

1. Routing and Remote Access Server offered in Windows 2000 is a very versatile service and will support the following VPN protocols: IPSec, PPTP, and L2TP. IPSec is a suite of cryptography-based protection services. It is used to provide machine-level authentication. PPTP is Microsoft's legacy protocol for supporting VPNs.

*For more information refer to the section on Components of Windows 2000 VPN in Chapter 5 of the **Windows 2000 Network Administration Study Guide.***

2. By configuring the Routing and Remote Access server to use callback, all the toll charges following the initial connection to the service will be on the company's bill, not the user's bill. After the initial connection, the service will call the user back and reconnect the user on the network. This type of procedure has been available for several years thus reducing costs by leveraging the company's more favorable long distance rates.

3. Use the Windows-Groups criteria and add the user to an authorized group. Launch the Routing and Remote Access console and create a Remote Access Policy. Associate her Security Group with the Remote Access policy, and ensure her dial-in permissions are set to Allow, or Control Access Through Remote Access Policy. If Control Access Through Remote Access Policy, grant her access in the permissions associated with the policy.

4. The only way to provide additional bandwidth other than offering a different access media is to engage Multilink and have the users add an additional modem and modem line on the remote end. This will allow the users to combine their bandwidth across two separate connections.

5. To determine raw numbers on bandwidth through the server, use the Performance console. Select the RAS Total Object and add the Total Bytes Received and Total Bytes Transmitted counters. The two counters added together will give you total additional traffic.

ANSWERS TO KEY TERM QUIZ

1. Multilink

2. Encryption

3. Authentication

4. Point-to-Point Protocol (PPP)

5. IPSec

6

Installing, Configuring, Managing, Monitoring, and Troubleshooting Network Protocols

Communication is the basis of any human relationship. It's the exchange or transmission of messages by speech or signals; using words effectively to impart information. An agreed upon language of common words or signals is such that it is understood between two people. So, too, must a protocol (agreed upon language) be installed on each network component before these components can communicate and understand the signals that are transmitted.

This lab chapter will focus on the two dominant protocol suites used today: TCP/IP (Transmission Control Protocol/Internet Protocol) and IPX/SPX (Internet Packet Exchange/Sequenced Packet Exchange), known in the Windows world environment as NWLink IPX/SPX.

The case scenarios in this lab chapter will address the issues of installing each protocol, configuring a static IP address; monitor IP network traffic; and install and configure NWLink IPX/SPX. There will also be a case study on using FTP (File Transfer Protocol) to access an FTP server and download a file.

LAB EXERCISE 6.01

Using FTP to Download a File

10 Minutes

Dr. Cutter in the Surgical Department calls you to say that, while he was using the Add/Remove Programs utility, he mistakenly deleted the anti-virus program on his computer. Apparently, he's been using his computer without virus protection for the past ten days. Can you come down and install a new copy? Your task is to download an anti-virus program onto Dr. Cutter's PC from the hospital's FTP site.

Learning Objectives

In this lab, you'll download files from an FTP site. By the end of this lab, you'll be able to:

■ Access and login to an FTP server

■ Get a directory listing showing the program file

■ Use the GET command to download the program file

Some people would consider this a bit archaic since the same can be accomplished using a web browser. But, sometimes breaking through all of the GUIs and using commands in a DOS environment provides for a quick and dirty process.

Lab Materials and Setup

This lab will require the following items:

- Two working computers
- Windows 2000 software (workstation and server with FTP services enabled)
- Network access to the FTP server

Getting Down to Business

To start the process of downloading the anti-virus program from the FTP site:

Step 1.   Access and log into an FTP server using a DOS session.

Step 2.   Open an FTP session with the server.

Step 3.   Use the GET command to download the program file.

Step 4.   Close the FTP session and exit DOS.

LAB EXERCISE 6.02

Discovering an IP Address on a Workstation   10 Minutes

Your next task is to look at a computer in the stat lab that cannot seem to log onto the Pixsys system on the Internet. The office manager that wrote up the incident report confirmed that the other computers in the lab are able to access the Internet. Your task is to examine the IP address and related information and make sure that they match the stat lab's assigned addresses.

Learning Objectives

In this lab, you'll troubleshoot a computer that is having trouble accessing the Internet. By the end of this lab, you will know how to:

■ Verify an IP address settings through the Networking and Dial-up Connections window.

Lab Material and Setup

This lab will require the following:

■ A working computer

■ Installed network card

■ Windows 2000 Professional software

Getting Down to Business

To verify that the static IP address and related information is configured correctly:

Step 1.   Launch the Local Area Connection Properties window through the Settings menu.

Step 2.   Select the TCP/IP protocol in the Components checked are used by this connection window.

Step 3.   Open the Internet Properties window.

Step 4.   Information in this window, the Internet Properties (TCP/IP) Properties window, will show whether the protocol's IP address information has been entered.

LAB EXERCISE 6.03

Subnetting Basics

15 Minutes

James from Bedrock Industries calls you for some help. He's trying to find the subnet of a particular computer that is having problems. He also wants to know the range of assignable IP addresses on this same subnet because it will be expanding to another floor in the same building.

He's at a complete loss as to how to figure it out. Because he took over the administrator's position three months ago, he can't find any documentation from the previous administrator on the six subnets within the company. James is asking for your help to solve this problem. You tell him to give you the IP address of the host and the subnet address for the network, and you'll calculate which subnet the host is on, and give him the IP address range.

Learning Objectives

In this lab exercise, your tasks are to figure out which subnet the host is on, and also calculate the IP address range for that subnet. Knowing the range of IP addresses will give you the number of computers (hosts) that can be connected to that subnet. By the of the lab, you will know how to:

- Convert IP address to binary
- Determine subnet address
- Determine range of assignable IP addresses on that subnet

Lab Materials and Setup

This lab requires a pencil, paper, and maybe a calculator.

Getting Down to Business

James has given you the following information from which to determine the subnet address of the host and the range of available IP addresses for that subnet.

■ IP address: 186.60.50.2

■ Subnet mask: 255.255.224.0

Step 1. You need to determine the subnet.

Perform a logical calculation on the IP address and the subnet mask.

Step 2. You need to find the range of IP addresses.

Take the result of the above calculation and compare it with the subnet mask.

LAB EXERCISE 6.04

15 Minutes

Installing and Configuring TCP/IP with a Static IP Address

Marge Gram-Stain, a pathology assistant in the Department of Medical Technology, needs a new computer installed in one of the labs on the 4th floor. You're job is to hook the new computer to the network. In this lab exercise, you'll need to configure the computer's static IP address so that it communicates with the network.

Learning Objectives

In this lab exercise, your task will be to set a computer's static IP address so that it communicates with the network. By the end of this lab, you will know how to:

■ Install TCP/IP

■ Configure TCP/IP with static IP address, subnet mask, and default gateway

Lab Materials and Setup

This lab will require the following:

- A working computer
- Installed network card
- Windows 2000 Professional software

You should also have a Windows 2000 Professional CD handy if you need to extract files not found on the hard drive. A live connection is not required to perform this lab.

Getting Down to Business

All the labs in the building have static IP addresses to identify computers on the network using the 3rd octet set. All lab computers have the number 230 as the 3rd octet set for ID purposes. The IP addressing parameters are:

- IP address range is 192.128.230.01 to 192.128.230.40
- The subnet mask is 255.255.0.0
- The gateway IP address is: 192.128.100.1
- No DNS and DHCP servers are being used

Step 1. Launch the Local Area Connection Properties window through the Settings menu.

Step 2. Check to see if the TCP/IP protocol is installed.

lab
(l)int *TCP/IP should have already been installed during the build process.*

Step 3. If you see TCP/IP in the list, skip to step 9.

Step 4. If TCP/IP is not in the list, click Install.

Step 5. The Selected Network Component Type dialog box opens.

Step 6. Select Protocol then click Add.

Step 7. Select TCP/IP and click OK.

Step 8. The window closes, returning you to the Local Area Connection Properties window.

lab
(hint *Now that you have installed, or verified, TCP/IP you need to configure TCP/IP.*

Step 9. Select the TCP/IP protocol in the Components Checked Are Used By This Connection window.

Step 10. Click Properties.

Step 11. To assign an IP address, activate the Use the Following IP Address radio button.

Step 12. In the IP address field, enter the assigned IP address for the computer.

lab
(hint *You already know three of the four octet sets; you just need to determine the last set.*

Step 13. In the Subnet Mask field, enter the assigned subnet mask number.

Step 14. In the Default Gateway field, enter the assigned gateway address.

Step 15. Click OK to accept these settings.

LAB EXERCISE 6.05

Installing Monitor and Gathering Network Statistics

20 Minutes

You receive a call from Josh, a junior administrator at Menn-Tall Hospital. They've had their segment of the network for only six months. Felix, the senior administrator, has asked him to install Network Monitor, the utility that captures packets sent back and forth from the server, and measures network utilization and other statistics. He's also been given the task of putting together a benchmark so Felix knows how the system should perform.

Learning Objectives

In this lab exercise, your task will show Josh how to install Network Monitor and how to set up a benchmark for the system. By the end of this lab, you will know how to:

- Install Network Monitor
- Launch Network Monitor
- Capture a benchmark set of statistics for the network

Lab Materials and Setup

- Two computers
- Windows 2000 software (workstation and server)
- Windows 2000 Professional CD
- Windows 2000 Server CD

You should have the CDs available if you need to extract files not found on the hard drive. A live connection is required to perform this lab.

Getting Down to Business

Step 1. Launch Add/Remove Programs from Control Panel.

Step 2. Click Add/Remove Windows Components.

Step 3. Select Management and Monitoring Tools.

Step 4. Once installed, click Finish.

Step 5. Launch the Monitor Tool from the Administration Tools Menu.

Step 6. Initiate a capture session to begin the benchmark process.

lab Hint *Capture three benchmark sessions during light traffic, medium traffic, and heavy traffic. Days and times will depend on the size and complexity of the network.*

Step 7. Save each benchmark session for comparison purposes.

LAB EXERCISE 6.06

Installing and Configuring NWLink

10 Minutes

Jim Pilladay from the pharmacy calls you. He has just received a laptop that he purchased for the department to use at the counter when servicing patients. Because he was anxious to use it, he connected the laptop to the system to access the patient database. He doesn't understand why he can't connect to it. He can connect to the Internet and the supply management database, but not the patient database. Could you help him with this problem?

Learning Objectives

Jim is not aware that the patient database is on a Novell NetWare Server. Although he can connect to the other services, his laptop does not have the IPX/SPX protocol installed. By the end of this lab you will be able to:

- Install and configure NWLink
- Install and configure Client Services for NetWare

Lab Materials and Setup

For this lab, you'll need the following:

- A working computer
- Installed network card
- Windows 2000 Professional software

Getting Down to Business

Step 1. Launch the Local Area Connection Properties window through the Settings menu.

Step 2. Click Install.

Step 3. Select Protocol.

Step 4. Click Add.

Step 5. Select NWLink.

Step 6. Configure the NWLink protocol.

Step 7. Click OK.

Step 8.   Install Client Services for NetWare.

Step 9.   Click Install.

Step 10.   Select Client.

Step 11.   Click Add.

Step 12.   Select Client Services for NetWare (CSNW).

Step 13.   Configure CSNW.

Step 14.   Click OK in the Local Area Connection Properties window.

LAB ANALYSIS TEST

1. While downloading an upgrade file on Dr. Cryle's computer, she asks you why you're using the FTP utility in DOS and not a web browser to download the file.

2. Jill, the office manager of the stat lab, wants to understand why a computer needs an IP address for it to communicate on the network.

3. Jim Pilladay still doesn't understand why he needs to have NWLink installed on the laptop to access the patient database. Give a brief explanation.

4. Explain to Josh from Menn-Tell Hospital what a network baseline is and why it is important to have one.

5. What are the three necessary elements in the Internet Properties (TCP/IP) Properties window in order for the computer to communicate over the network?

KEY TERM QUIZ

Use the following vocabulary terms to complete the sentences below. Not all of the terms will be used.

FTP

TCP/IP

IP address

Protocol

NWLink

Gateway

Subnet mask

Frame type

Network binding

baseline

1. The default Microsoft network protocol _____, is a communications suite.

2. If you wish to allow a Windows operating system to communicate with a Novell NetWare system you would install _____, which uses the IPX/SPX protocol.

3. _____ is a standard TCP/IP protocol component that allows you to transfer files.

4. The _____ is used to identify a TCP/IP host's network and ID.

5. An agreed upon format to transmit data between two devices is called a _____.

LAB WRAP-UP

Let's recap the topics covered in the chapter. We've seen the importance of networking protocols. It's these protocols that allow components to communicate over a network. We saw how FTP, part of the TCP/IP suite, is used to download a file. We verified, installed, and configured an IP address. We installed monitoring software on our server to view network packets being transmitted over the network. Lastly, we installed and configured NWLink and CSNW so that our Windows network could communicate with a Novell network.

One other lesson to be learned here is that, with any network of computers, effective planning, monitoring, and early stage troubleshooting keeps a system on-line and trouble-free.

LAB SOLUTIONS FOR CHAPTER 6

In this section, you'll find solutions to the lab exercises, Lab Analysis Test, and Key Term Quiz.

Lab Solution 6.01

Downloading via FTP is a straightforward procedure. With the FTP protocol embedded in web browsers, it's not used as much. But, it is a handy tool to have if the site is not running a web service.

Be sure that when downloading a file using FTP that you are in the directory where you wish to download into. For example, if you are downloading the file into My Downloaded Files folder, your pointer should show: c:\my downloaded files.

Step. 1. Open a DOS session.

Step 2. Type FTP at the command line.

Step 3. Open an FTP session with the server (OPEN *server*). Provide username and password if required.

Step 4. Use the CD command to change directories to the location of the file (CD *directoryname*).

Step 5. Use the DIR command to browse the directory to find the file.

Step 6. Switch FTP to binary mode with the bin command if the file is an executable.

Step 7. Use the GET command to download the program file (GET *filename*).

Step 8. Close the FTP session, quit FTP, and close the DOS session.

Lab Solution 6.02

In this lab, you're verifying a computer's IP address settings through the Networking and Dial-up Connections window.

To verify that the static IP address and related information is configured correctly:

Step 1. Launch the Local Area Connection Properties window through the Settings menu.

Step 2. Select the TCP/IP protocol in the Components Checked Are Used By This Connection window.

Step 3. Click Properties.

Step 4. Information in this window, the Internet Properties (TCP/IP) Properties window, will show whether the protocol's IP address information has been entered.

This screenshot, as shown in Figure 6-1, shows a network that uses a static IP address rather than have each computer receive an IP address from what is known as a DHCP (Dynamic Host Configuration Protocol) server. What you are looking for is the correct IP address numbers, the correct subnet mask, and a gateway address if one is being used. A misplaced number can cause a computer not to connect.

Lab Solution 6.03

This lab exercise can be a challenge if you're new to subnetting. It's definitely not for the faint of heart. Yet, it's something that needs to be learned as an administrator.

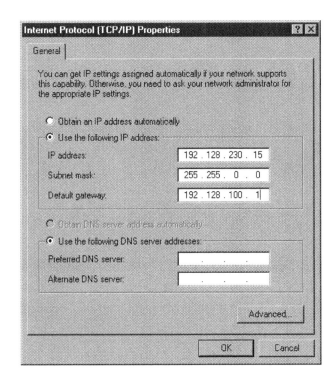

In this lab exercise, your task was to figure out which subnet the host is on, calculate the IP address range for that subnet, and use binary numbers to solve it with. Knowing the range IP addresses will give you the number of computers (hosts) that can be connected to that subnet. By the end of the lab, you will know how to:

- Convert IP address to binary
- Determine subnet address
- Determine range of assignable IP addresses on that subnet

James has given you the following information from which to determine the subnet address of the host and the range of available IP addresses for that subnet.

- IP address: 186.60.50.2
- Subnet mask: 255.255.224.0

Before we perform any calculations we need to convert the third octet into binary.

Step 1.   You need to determine the subnet.

	128	64	32	16	8	4	2	1
50 =	0	0	1	1	0	0	1	0
224 =	1	1	1	0	0	0	0	0

We compare the two binary numbers and eliminate all except the positions where there is a one. This happens to be position 32. Therefore the value is 32. The subnet that the host resides is 186.60.32.0. There was no need to address the first two octets (186.60) because that represents the network ID.

Step 2.   You need to find the range of IP addresses.
We again compare the results of the above calculation with the subnet mask that will give us the end of the subnet range.

	128	64	32	16	8	4	2	1
32 =	0	0	1	0	0	0	0	0
224 =	1	1	1	0	0	0	0	0

As we look at the binary number, the bits that are converted by the mask will be left alone. The rest of the bits, we will convert to 1s. This results in:

	128	64	32	16	8	4	2	1	
	0	0	1	1	1	1	1	1	= 63

Thus, the range for assignable IP addresses on the subnet 186.60.32.0 is 186.60.32.1 to 186.60.63.254. Remember, we figured out what the subnet is, 32, and then figured out the range, 63.

Lab Solution 6.04

In this lab exercise, your task was to set a computer's static IP address so that it communicates with the network. The previous lab assumes that the TCP/IP protocol had been installed during installation. In this lab you needed to install the TCP/IP protocol and set the correct IP, subnet mask, and gateway addresses.

You were given the following information: All the labs in the building have static IP addresses to identify computers on the network using the 3rd octet set. All lab computers have the number 230 as the 3rd octet set for ID purposes. The IP addressing parameters are:

- IP address range is 192.128.230.01 to 192.128.230.40
- The subnet mask is 255.255.0.0
- The gateway IP address is: 192.128.100.1
- No DNS and DHCP servers are being used

Step 1. Launch the Local Area Connection Properties window through the Settings menu.

Step 2. Check to see if the TCP/IP protocol is installed, as shown in Figure 6-2. If TCP/IP had not been installed then it would not show in the components list.

FIGURE 6-2

Check here to see if the TCP/IP component is installed

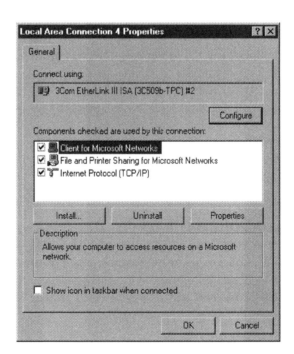

Step 3.   If TCP/IP is not in the list, click Install.

Step 4.   A dialog box titled Selected Network Component Type opens.

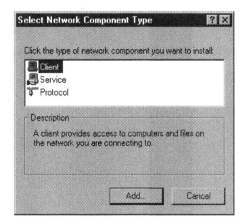

Step 5.   Select Protocol; click Add.

Step 6.   Select TCP/IP and click OK.

Step 7.   The window closes, returning you to the Local Area Connection Properties window, as shown in Figure 6-3.
Now that you have installed, or verified, TCP/IP you need to configure TCP/IP.

Step 8.   Select the TCP/IP protocol in the Components Checked Are Used By This Connection window.

Step 9.   Click Properties.

Step 10.   To assign an IP address, activate the Use The Following IP Address radio button.

Step 11.   In the IP address field, enter the assigned IP address for the computer.

lab
ⓘint
You already know three of the four octet sets; you just need to determine the last set.

FIGURE 6-3

Locate the installed TCP/IP protocol in in the window

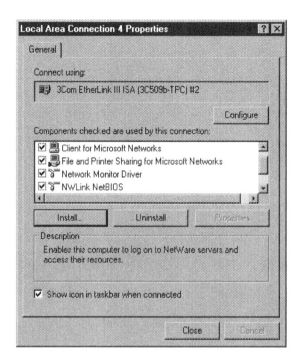

Step 12. In the Subnet Mask field enter the assigned subnet mask number, as shown in Figure 6-4.

Step 13. In the Default Gateway field enter the assigned gateway address, as shown in Figure 6-5.

Step 14. Clicking OK will install these settings.

Lab Solution 6.05

In this lab exercise, your task was to show Josh how to install Network Monitor, and how to setup a benchmark for the system.

Step 1. Launch Add/Remove Programs from the Control Panel menu.

Step 2. Click the Add/Remove Windows Components button as shown in Figure 6-6.

FIGURE 6-4

Enter the IP
address, Subnet
Mask, and
Gateway in this
properties
window

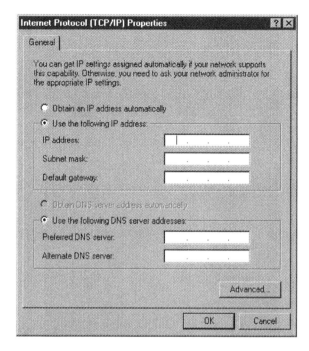

FIGURE 6-5

This is what the
entries should
look like

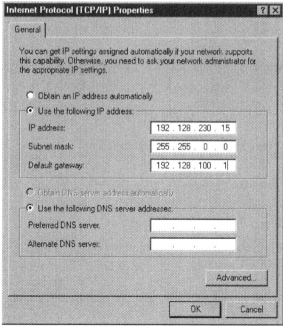

FIGURE 6-6

Click the
Add/Remove
Windows
Components to
install Network
Monitor

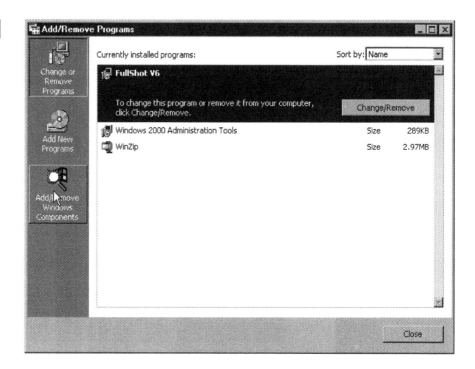

Step 3. Select Management and Monitoring Tools as shown in Figure 6-7.

Step 4. Once installed, click Finish. Installing Network Monitor also installs the Network Monitor driver. This driver is necessary so that the SMS (Storage Management Service) can retrieve those packets that are sent to and from this network adapter.

Step 5. Launch the Monitor Tool from the Administration Tools menu.

Step 6. Initiate a capture session to begin the benchmark process.

Step 7. Click Capture from the menu bar.

Step 8. Select Start. This actives the monitoring process.

Step 9. To freeze a particular moment select Stop from Capture on the menu bar.

FIGURE 6-7

Be sure that the
Management and
Monitoring Tools
utilities is checked

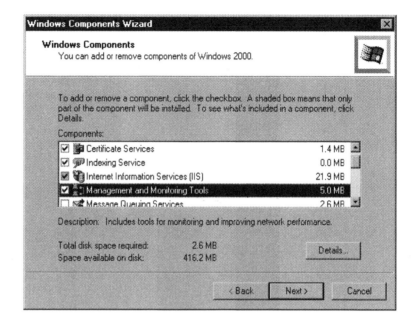

Step 10.   Click Start from Capture on the menu bar to resume. Whenever you stop and then select Start again, it will ask you if you want to save the session.

Step 11.   To save session click OK and you will be given a window in which to save the session.

Step 12.   Click OK to save the session and a new session will start as shown in Figure 6-8.

Capturing benchmarks for your system involves tracking packet (frame) transmission during a certain time period. Light traffic time is normally during the lunch period; medium traffic, normally during the 9:30 A.M. to 11:30 A.M. or 2 P.M. to 4 P.M. time period; heavy traffic, normally during the initial login period in the morning or logoff period. Another heavy traffic example may be during a payroll batch process or database query. When to run your benchmark captures will depend on the size and complexity of the network. The utility allows you to save each session so you can compare it with other sessions.

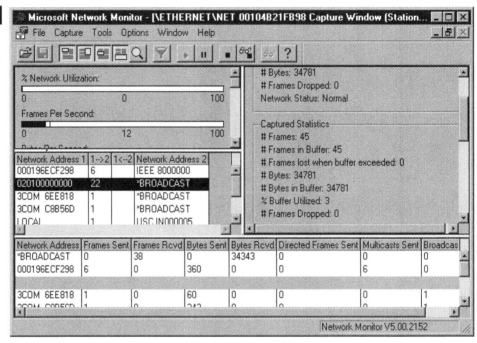

FIGURE 6-8

This is how the Monitor Window appears after starting a session

Lab Solution 6.06

Jim Pilladay, the pharmacist, thought he knew enough about computers to connect his laptop to the network. His didn't realize that the laptop did not have the IPX/SPX protocol installed. In this lab exercise you needed to:

- Install and configure NWLink
- Install and configure Client Services for NetWare

Step 1. Launch the Local Area Connection Properties window through the Settings menu.

Step 2. Click Install.

Step 3. Select Protocol.

Step 4. Click Add.

Step 5. Select NWLink, as shown in Figure 6-9.

Step 6. Configure the NWLink protocol.

Step 7. Click OK.

Step 8. Install the Client Services for NetWare.

Step 9. Click Install.

Step 10. Select Client.

Step 11. Click Add.

Step 12. Select Client Services for NetWare (CSNW), as shown in Figure 6-10.

Step 13. Configure CSNW. The easiest way of setting IPX/SPX is to have the system locate the appropriate frame type (auto frame type detection), as shown in Figure 6-11. If you're positive of the frame type and network number of the NetWare system then you can enter them in.

FIGURE 6-9

Install NWLink from this window

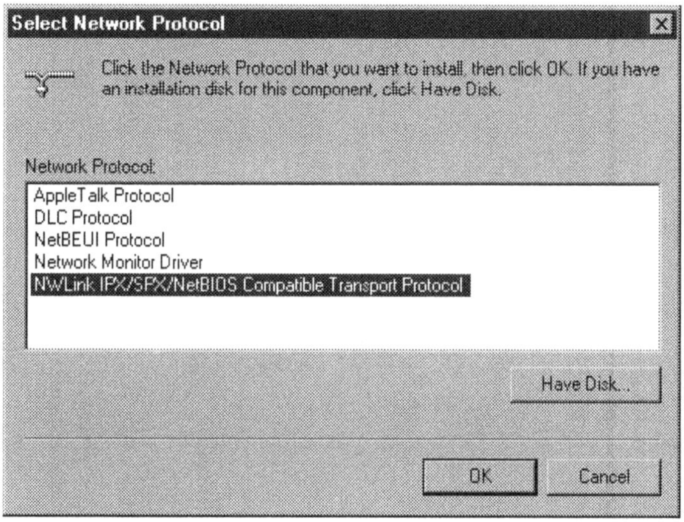

FIGURE 6-10

Select the
NetWare Client
Services here

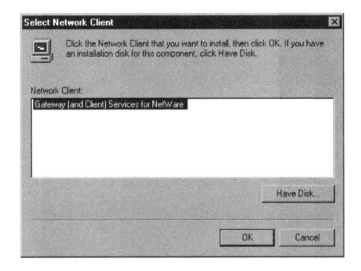

FIGURE 6-11

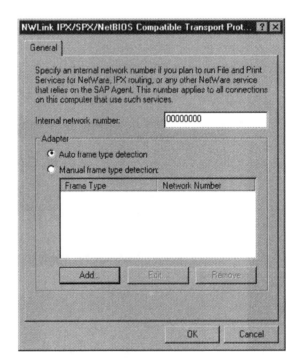

ANSWERS TO LAB ANALYSIS TEST

1. File Transfer Protocol (FTP) is used to transfer files between computers. Computers that share these files may not be a complex system that is also running a web server and providing links to those files.

2. An IP address is a series of numbers that represents a computer on a network. Each computer that needs connectivity on a TCP/IP network needs to have its own unique address.

3. NWLink is Microsoft's version of Novell's IPX/SPX protocol used to communicate with a NetWare server.

4. A baseline is a set of network performance readings, captured at certain times of the day or week, and used to reference future readings to see if any changes in performance, beyond the norm, are occurring.

5. In order to communicate over the network, the following elements are needed: IP address, used to identify the computer on the network; Subnet Mask, used to determine what subdivision of a network an IP address belongs to; and Gateway, the address of the router which the packets from a computer should use to leave a network subdivision.

ANSWERS TO KEY TERM QUIZ

1. TCP/IP
2. NWLink
3. FTP
4. IP address
5. Protocol

7

Configuring and Troubleshooting IP Security

I P Security (IPSec), an extension of the IP protocol, is a framework of open standards for ensuring private communication over IP networks. It provides point-to-point encryption of data between two computers.

In this chapter we will look at the security features of IPSec and Layer 2 Tunneling Protocol (L2TP) on a network. We'll also look at enabling, implementing, configuring, and managing of the security protocol known as IPSec.

LAB EXERCISE 7.01

IPSec and L2TP Security

10 Minutes

Your consulting firm, Fortress Computing Inc., provides services for a prominent downtown financial institution. The company uses TCP/IP on a Windows 2000 network. Their domain consists of 12 domain controllers and 750 Windows 2000 Professional computers. Most of the users connect via leased lines to their offices. Brad, the security manager needs to understand why you've suggested implementing IPSec and L2TP to secure data transmission between all locations.

Learning Objectives

When utilizing a Virtual Private Network, you want to establish the most secure connection possible. The combination of IP Security and L2TP provides a highly secured tunnel between two points. The original packet header carries the packet source and destination information. IPSec is used to secure the tunnel, and L2TP header carries information needed for routing the packet over the network. By the end of this lab, you will be able to:

■ Understand IPSec and L2TP security

Lab Materials and Setup

For this lab exercise, you'll need:

■ Pencil and paper
■ Windows 2000 Professional Server

Getting Down to Business

To produce a report to distribute to the committee you need to first compose a list of benefits for IPSec and another for L2TP.

Step 1. Write a brief explanation that will be distributed to the planning committee to explain why implementing IPSec and L2TP for all computers is the best solution for the company.

_____

_____

LAB EXERCISE 7.02

Enabling and Configuring IPSec

15 Minutes

You are the network administrator of Warwick Energy, a company that employs marketing representatives who call on businesses in the area to offer the companies products and services. These representatives are not required to report to the office each day, so they operate out of their houses. They connect to the network daily to retrieve the contacts for the day and to transmit client contracts. Because of the confidential information transmitted back to the office, you need to ensure a secure connection between the representative and the home office. What security policy would you implement on the server and on the representative's computers?

Learning Objectives

Prior to enabling IPSec on a local computer or domain, you'll want to configure IPSec using policies. In this lab, you'll set rules that define how and when security is set between two points. By the end of this lab, you will be able to:

- Use the Microsoft Management Console (MMC)
- Add the IP Security (IPSec) Snap-in
- Create an IP security policy

These security policies are created for the most common communication scenarios. Once created, these policies are stored in directory services and then assigned to domain policies.

Lab Material and Setup

This lab will require the following:

- A working computer
- Installed network card
- Windows 2000 Professional Server software

Getting Down to Business

To begin the activation of IPSec through a policy, perform the following:

Step 1. Type MMC /s in the Run window of the Start button. This will launch Microsoft's Management Console with an "s" switch. This switch designates Snap-in.

Step 2. Select Add/Remove Snap-in from the Console menu.

Step 3. Choose and add the IP Security Policy Management item from the list of components.

Step 4. Click Local Computer in the next window. The snap-in will create an IPSec Policy Management component for the computer on which the console is running. Take note of the other options available to you.

Step 5. Click Finish and complete the process.

Step 6. Right-click IP Security Policies, and select Create IP Security Policy. The IP Security Policy Wizard starts.

Step 7. Enter a description and policy name in the IP Security Policy Name window.

Step 8. The Activate The Default Response Rule is automatically selected in the Requests For Secure Communication window. This is where the policy will be set as the default policy for any secure communications requests.

Step 9. The Default Response Rule Authentication Method window lets you configure the default rule of authentication for secure communications requests. What default protocol is set as the Windows 2000 default for an authentication protocol?

Step 10. Clicking Next brings you to the Complete The IP Security Policy Wizard window. You now have the option to edit the policy properties.

Step 11. End the wizard and move on to the Security Policy Properties window.

Step 12. Return to the console screen. The new policy is now listed in the right pane.

Step 13. Assign the policy and change the entry from No to Yes.

LAB EXERCISE 7.03

Managing, Monitoring, and Troubleshooting IPSec

5 Minutes

As a network administrator for a distance learning training center, you need to periodically check the secure connections between students and the network over the Internet. What monitoring tool provides a quick and succinct view of traffic speed, length of connection, and bytes transferred in and out of the system?

Learning Objectives

Unlike the other Windows 2000 components that can be tracked with System Monitor, use IPSec Monitor to confirm if your secured communications are successful. It displays the active security associations on local or remote computers. In this lab exercise, your task is to monitor the connection between the two computers. By the of the lab, you will know how to:

■ Look at monitoring information for an IPSec Security Association

Lab Materials and Setup

This lab will require the following:

■ A working computer
■ Installed network card
■ Windows 2000 Professional Server software

Getting Down to Business

To monitor an IPSec secure connection perform the following:

Step 1. Choose Run from the Start menu.

Step 2. Type **ipsecmon** *Payroll,* where *Payroll* is the computer that you want to monitor.

Step 3. Click Options to set the refresh rate.

LAB ANALYSIS TEST

1. You are the network administrator for E. A. Adams Business Office Products. Your Windows 2000 network has grown to include two domain controllers and 150 Windows 2000 Professional computers. You've decided it is time to implement Microsoft's native Kerberos V5 security protocol. What steps are needed to implement the authentication protocol?

_____

_____

2. Maria is the network administrator for Granite State Insurance Company. She has called you because she is in the middle of setting up VPN connections for the company's independent agents. She is trying to create a secure environment when the agents connect to the office. What must you do to enable IPSec policy on the computers?

_____

_____

3. Maria is not clear on the function of IPSec policy. She would like you to explain the responsibility of the IPSec policy agent?

_____

_____

4. Your distribution company, which is based in Albany, NY, has just acquired another distribution firm that has an office in New Orleans. Both offices are composed of Windows 2000 domains. The new office connects to the Internet using a fractional T1 line. Your task is to provide a secure connection between the two sites. Data security and price are an issue. What solution would you offer?

_____

_____

5. Jeff, the senior MCSE in Fits-Like-a-Glove Mfg., is having a discussion with Vinny, the LAN administrator, on the differences between the PPTP and L2TP when creating VPNs on the network. What advantage would L2TP have over PPTP?

_____

_____

KEY TERM QUIZ

Use the following vocabulary terms to complete the sentences below. Not all of the terms will be used.

     IPSec

     Kerberos V5

     Tunneling

     Public key certificate

     Certificate

     Public key infrastructure

     Cryptography

     Data encryption standard

     Authentication

     Baseline

1. The process that verifies the user's appropriate rights or permissions to access resources on a network is called _____.

2. The science of encrypting and decrypting data is _____. It ensures confidentiality, data integrity, and authentication.

3. _____ provides for encryption of data as it travels between two clients. It protects it from modification and interpretation from network snooping.

4. An Internet security protocol used for handling authenticating users, _____ encrypts passwords that are sent across network connections.

5. _____ is a term generally used to describe the standards and software that regulate digital certificates, and public & private keys.

LAB WRAP-UP

Let's recap the topics covered in the chapter. We've seen how IPSec polices and rules are enabled and implemented on a network. We've also looked at the security features of IPSec and L2TP on a network. Since IPSec is installed by default, what you need to do is enable it through the MMC console using the IP Security Management Snap-in and assign policies to be used on the network. We've also seen how to monitor IPSec Security Associations using ipsecmon.

LAB SOLUTIONS FOR CHAPTER 7

In this section, you'll find solutions to the lab exercises, Lab Analysis Test, and Key Term Quiz.

Lab Solution 7.01

Implementing IPSec and L2TP for all computers, including dial-up computers, will secure data and ensure that only authorized packets will access the network resources. IPSec is a set of open standards that guarantees secure, private transfer of data over an IP network.

Lab Solution 7.02

Prior to enabling IPSec on a local computer or domain, you want to configure IPSec using policies. In this lab, you set rules that define how and when security is set between two points. By the end of this lab, you were able to:

■ Use the Microsoft Management Console (MMC)

■ Add the IP Security (IPSec) Snap-in

■ Create an IP security policy

These security policies are created for the most common communication scenarios. Once created, these policies are stored in directory services and then assigned to domain policies.

To begin the activation of IPSec through a policy, perform the following:

Step 1. Click Start | Run.

Step 2. Type **MMC /s** in the Run window. This will launch Microsoft's Management Console with an "s" switch. This switch designates Snap-in.

Step 3. Select Add/Remove Snap-in from the Console menu as seen in Figure 7-1. The dialog box appears where you can add a Snap-in.

Step 4. Choose and add the IP Security Policy Management item from the list of components as shown in Figure 7-2.

FIGURE 7-1

A snap-in is an
operating system
modules that can
be plugged-in or
out

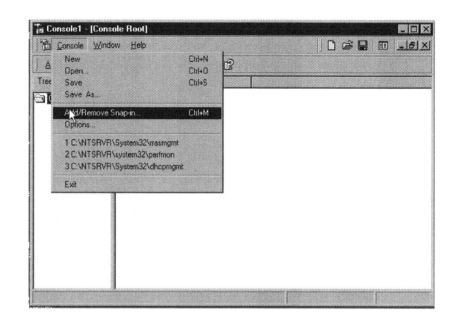

FIGURE 7-2

More than one
component can
be added to the
MMC

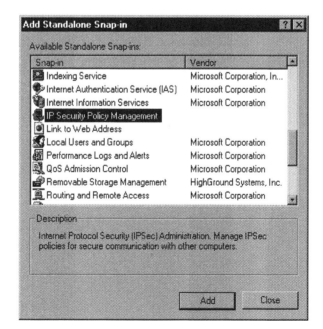

Step 5. Your next screen has you select the computer which the Snap-in will manage. Click Local Computer. The Snap-in will create an IPSec Policy Management component for the computer where the console is running. Take note of the other options available to you.

Step 6. Click Finish, then Close, and OK to return to MMC.

Step 7. To configure the IP Security Policy, right-click the IP Security Policies and select Create IP Security Policy. The policy wizard starts.

Step 8. Click Next to open the IP Security Policy Name window. Enter a description and policy name.

Step 9. Open the Requests For Secure Communication window. This defines the default policy rule for any secure communications requests. The Activate The Default Response Rule is automatically selected as shown in Figure 7-3.

This dialog box shows the default response rule for the default policy

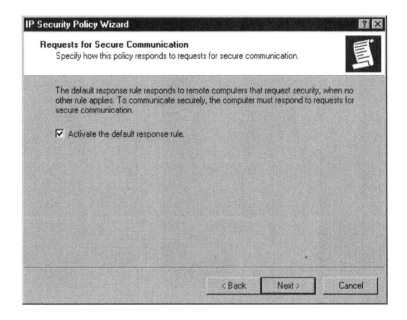

Step 10.   Clicking Next will open the Default Response Rule Authentication Method window. This window lets you configure the default rule of authentication for secure communications requests. Automatically, the Windows 2000 default (Kerberos V5 Protocol) is active as shown in Figure 7-4.

Step 11.   Clicking Next brings you to the Complete The IP Security Policy Wizard window. You now have the option to edit the policy properties.

Step 12.   Click Finish to end the wizard and go to the Security Policy Properties window.

Step 13.   Click OK to close the properties window and return to the Console screen. The new policy is now listed in the right pane.

Step 14.   Activate the policy by right clicking the policy and select Assign. This will activate the policy and change the entry from No to Yes.

This dialog box allows you to configure the security level of data requests and how they will authenticate

Lab Solution 7.03

Unlike the other Windows 2000 components that can be tracked with System Monitor, Use IPSec Monitor to confirm if your secured communications are successful. It displays the active security associations on local or remote computers. In this lab exercise, your task is to monitor the connection between the two computers. By the end of the lab, you were able to:

■   Look at monitoring information for the IPSec port.

To monitor an IPSec secure connection perform the following:

Step 1.   Choose Run from the Start menu.

Step 2.   Type **ipsecmon** *Payroll*, where *Payroll* is the computer that you want to monitor.

Step 3.   View the available statistics in the IP Security Monitor window as show in Figure 7-5.

FIGURE 7-5

This tool monitors security polices, packets and bytes activity

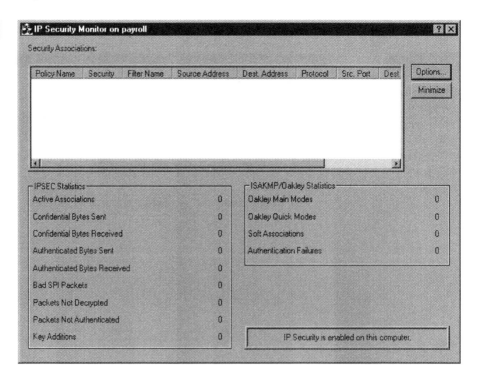

Step 4. Click Options to set the refresh rate.

ANSWERS TO LAB ANALYSIS TEST

1. Since Kerberos V5 is a default security protocol for Windows 2000, it is already enabled when you install a domain controller.

2. IPSec components are installed by default when Windows 2000 is built. To enable IPSec you need to create a custom console using the MMC that includes the IP Security Policy Management Snap-in, and then use the Snap-in to assign policies.

3. The policy agent is responsible for retrieving the computer's assigned IPSec policy from the Active Directory.

4. You would consider connecting the two domains with a VPN. By implementing IPSec and L2TP, the data will be encrypted and free from deciphering between the two sites.

5. L2TP supports header compression, whereas PPTP does not. L2TP supports tunnel authentication, PPTP does not. And, L2TP requires IPsec for encryption, PPTP does not.

ANSWERS TO KEY TERM QUIZ

1. Authentication
2. Cryptography
3. IPSec
4. Kerberos V5
5. Public Key Infrastructure

MICROSOFT CERTIFIED SYSTEMS ENGINEER

8

Installing, Configuring, Managing, Monitoring, and Troubleshooting WINS

LAB EXERCISES

I n Windows 2000 networks only, the preferred method of name resolution is DNS. In the real world, however, most networks consist of a mixed bag of computers running various flavors of the Windows operating system: Windows 95, 98, NT, ME, XP, or Windows 2000. These networks must support the NetBIOS name to IP address name resolution. Windows Internet Name Service (WINS) is the system that provides that conversion.

In this chapter we will look at installing WINS using the Network and Dial-up Connections Properties window. We'll also configure the WINS installation by setting parameters on the Server Properties window. These include, among others, setting intervals in which records are renewed, deleted, and verified. We will cover the steps necessary to plan and implement a WINS solution, the issues that will arise when operating in a mixed environment, and what tools are available to monitor and troubleshoot WINS.

LAB EXERCISE 8.01

Installing WINS

10 Minutes

You're a systems consultant for EPROM Computing Consultants of Kentucky. This morning you're called to a client that operates a small auto body parts and paint distribution company in the state with six locations. Each location has a host computer. They've been in the process of upgrading the host systems to Windows 2000 but wish to make sure that their 2-year-old Windows NT 4 computers can browse the network. What solution would you offer to accomplish the request?

Learning Objectives

Because of the mixed operating system environment, Windows 2000 and Windows NT 4.0, the solution is to install WINS. At this point you are very much aware that many, if not all, installations are wizard driven. WINS is no exception. In this lab we will install WINS using the Network and Dial-up Connections Properties. By the end of this lab, you'll be able to:

■ Install Windows Internet Naming Service (WINS)

Lab Materials and Setup

For this lab exercise, you'll need:

- A working computer
- Installed network card
- Windows 2000 Server software

Getting Down to Business

To begin the installation process, perform the following:

Step 1. Select Properties from My Network Places.

Step 2. Click Add Network Components in the lower left corner to open the Optional Networking Components Windows Wizard.

Step 3. Choose Network Services and make sure that the WINS component is checked.

Step 4. Start the wizard to install WINS.

lab
Warning *The wizard may prompt you for the Windows 2000 CD if files need to be copied.*

Step 5. At the end of the wizard click OK to complete the process.

LAB EXERCISE 8.02

Configuring WINS

15 Minutes

Staying with the same case study as Lab Exercise 8.01 where you install WINS, you need to configure it for optimal performance. Based on the type and size of business, you've determined that the WINS parameters need to be adjusted from their default settings.

Learning Objectives

A number of properties can be configured in the WINS. These properties set the environment that WINS will operate. A knowledge of setting and modifying these properties ensures proper function of the service. By the end of this lab, you'll be able to:

- Set statistic updates
- Set intervals in which records are renewed, deleted, and verified
- Set database verification
- Activate the event log
- Set the request handling number

Lab Material and Setup

This lab will require the following:

- A working computer
- Installed network card
- Windows 2000 Server software

Getting Down to Business

To reach the properties window and make changes to those properties, perform the following:

Step 1.   Open the WINS Console.

Step 2.   Access the Properties window for the server you wish to configure.

Step 3.   In the General tab set the Automatically Update Statistics for every 10 minutes.

Step 4. In the Intervals tab set the following rates at which records will be renewed, deleted, and verified:

- Renew interval: 7 days
- Extinction interval: 5 days
- Extinction timeout: 7 days
- Verification interval: 30 days

Step 5. In the Database Verification tab, ensure that the consistency of the database is verified every 24 hours. It should be set at 2 hours, and the maximum number of records verified to the originating server is equal to 30,000.

Step 6. In the Advanced window, activate the event log and set the level of WINS requests that the server will accept to Medium.

lab
Hint *Burst Handling sets the number of WINS requests that the server will accept before a retry message is announced.*

Step 7. Click OK to close the window and apply your settings.

LAB EXERCISE 8.03

Planning and Implementing a WINS Solution

10 Minutes

You are the WAN administrator for the prestigious Bella Donna Boutiques. There are eight satellite locations, all connected with low-bandwidth WAN connections to the home office. Each location has its own WINS server for name resolution, and each WINS server will need to have replication capabilities. How would you configure the WINS replication from the home office WINS server to those in each of the eight boutiques?

Learning Objectives

As in any aspect of networking, redundancy/duplication is an important element to a healthy network, especially when it comes to database information and name resolution. You want to ensure that if the primary database ever becomes corrupt, you have a backup copy. Or, if you manage a large network with many users and/or a network that encompasses a large territory, or spans several states or countries, you have redundant WINS database to handle the queries. By the end of the lab, you will know how to:

- Configure WINS replication
- Restrict replication to replication partners only
- Set the Replication Partners Properties
- Enable a Push Replication to the Partner Server

Lab Materials and Setup

This lab will require the following:

- A working computer
- Installed network card
- Windows 2000 Server software

Getting Down to Business

To enable WINS replication, perform the following:

Step 1. Open the WINS console.

Step 2. Select your server. Right-click Replication Partners and select New Replication Partner.

Step 3. In the WINS server field of the dialog window, enter the name or IP address of another WINS server. You can also use the Browse button to search and select the WINS server.

lab
Hint

This lab portion requires a second WINS server running on the network. If this is not possible, then you may browse and enter your WINS server. The system will not allow the same database to partner with itself. You can still perform the steps to become familiar with the screens and prompts.

Step 4. Right click Replication Partners on the left side of the window and select Properties. This window has four tabs that need to be configured.

Step 5. In the General tab restrict replication-to-replication partners only.

Step 6. Select the Push Replication tab. Here we'll establish replication at service startup and when the address changes. We'll also allow for persistent connections for push replication partners.

Step 7. Once you complete adjusting the settings, click OK to have the settings take effect.

LAB EXERCISE 8.04

5 Minutes

Dealing with Interoperability Issues; Configuring TCP/IP to Use WINS

Joyce administers a Windows network for the Acme Brass Works Company. The Windows 2000 Server has several Windows 95 and Windows 98 clients. DHCP is configured on the server, and the WINS address is configured on the client computers. She gets a call from Mario to report that he cannot communicate with the network. At his computer she performs some troubleshooting. She pings the server and launches Internet Explorer to connect to a web site. Both tests succeed. Mario does admit that he has been in the TCP/IP Properties screen practicing what he's been learning at the Windows 2000 training class for end users. Joyce now has to fix the problem.

Learning Objectives

WINS clients register their computer names with a WINS server when they boot up and connect to the network. Clients then query the WINS server to resolve remote client names. Some of the client-to-WINS server functions include renewing client names with the WINS database and resolving client names by obtaining IP address mappings from the WINS database for user names, NetBIOS names, and NetBIOS services. By the end of the lab, you will know how to:

■ Configure TCP/IP to use WINS

Lab Materials and Setup

This lab will require the following:

■ A working computer

■ Installed network card

■ Windows 2000 Professional software

Getting Down to Business

To configure the WINS client to use the WINS server on Joyce's network, perform the following:

Step 1. Right-click the network connection you want to configure, and then click Properties.

Step 2. On the General tab access the Properties screen of Internet Protocol (TCP/IP).

Step 3. Click Advanced, click the WINS tab, and then click Add.

Step 4. Type the IP address, 192.168.32.1, of the WINS server in the TCP/IP WINS Server window, and then click Add.

lab
①int

The use of the Lmhosts file to resolve remote NetBIOS names is enabled by default.

Step 5.   Click OK and complete the process.

lab
Warning   *After completing the above procedure, the client will no longer have a*
dynamic (DHCP-assigned) WINS server address.

LAB EXERCISE 8.05

Monitoring and Troubleshooting WINS

10 Minutes

You are the network administrator of Backup Delight, a manufacturer of uninterrupted power supply and surge protector products. Your network consists of 150 Windows NT 4 client workstations connected to a Windows 2000 system. You are concerned that there are computers coming on the network with the same NetBIOS name. Your other concern you wish to check is the number of client computers that are adding updates to the WINS database. Which counters would you consider tracking in System Monitor to achieve your goal?

Learning Objectives

Ensuring an efficient system requires periodic monitoring of various Windows 2000 components. WINS is no exception. This scenario requires that you view three of these counters, Unique Conflicts/Sec, Total Number of Registrations/Sec, and Total Number of Renewals/Sec. The conflicts per second would show you if there are computers causing name conflicts. And, by tracking the additional two counters above, you'll capture both connected and new client computers that are registering with the server. By the end of the lab, you will know how to:

▪ Monitor Windows 2000 WINS services.

Lab Materials and Setup

This lab will require the following:

▪ A working computer

▪ Installed network card

▪ Windows 2000 Server software

Getting Down to Business

To monitor WINS services perform the following:

Step 1.   Open the Performance window and select System Monitor from the left side of split screen .

Step 2.   Open the Add Counters window.

Step 3.   Select the WINS Server in the Performance Object window. A list of counters will display in the window below. Select:

- Unique Conflicts/Sec
- Total Number of Registrations/Sec
- Total Number of Renewals/Sec

Step 4.   Add each of the counters above to monitor.

Step 5.   Click Close when done.

LAB ANALYSIS TEST

1. You are the network administrator for a small auto quick lube company with several sites in the state, each with a host computer. You're upgrading the hosts to Windows 2000, but you want to make sure that the Windows NT 4 computers can still connect and browse the network. What solution would you offer?

_____

_____

2. The Creature Comfort pet store has grown over the past two years to a five-location chain. There are WINS servers at the five locations, and as the systems administrator you wish to have them automatically replicate with each other. How would you accomplish this?

_____

_____

3. As the LAN administrator for Puddle Jumper Airline, one of your added duties is to train a junior administrator to help you maintain the network. She is having a hard time understanding the different NetBIOS node types being used, especially the type that Windows 2000 Professional uses. What is the default node used with Windows 2000 and explain its function?

_____

_____

4. You are the network administrator of Tollgate Enterprise. A Windows 2000 Server is installed at the corporate headquarters, but a mix of Windows 2000 and Windows NT computers connect to the server. For backward compatibility, WINS has been deployed, but you are unsure whether WINS is actually doing its job. How you find out?

_____

_____

5. You have successfully implemented WINS on your network environment, and all is working well. Your users can browse the network. How does the WINS database get populated to make browsing the network possible?

_____

_____

KEY TERM QUIZ

Use the following vocabulary terms to complete the sentences below. Not all of the terms will be used.

> transmission control
>
> LAN Manager HOSTS (LMHOSTS)
>
> B-node
>
> H-node
>
> M-node
>
> pull replication
>
> push replication
>
> WINS
>
> broadcasts
>
> tombstoned

1. Once a WINS entry is marked for deletion, it is considered _____ until it is actually deleted.

2. _____ is a Windows 2000 service that provides NetBIOS name resolution.

3. The NetBIOS node type that uses broadcasts to resolve NetBIOS names to IP addresses is named _____.

4. The act of replicating a copy of the WINS database is named _____.

5. _____ provides a static NetBIOS name to IP address resolution in a Windows environment.

LAB WRAP-UP

In this lab chapter we performed the installation and configuration of WINS on our server. The install is wizard-driven and configuration consists mainly of parameter settings for our network environment. We looked at implementing a WINS solution, using the replication process to ensure database availability on multiple server networks. We've configured TCP/IP to use WINS as a source for IP address resolution. Lastly, we added several counters to our System Monitor utility to check and monitor performance issues with WINS.

LAB SOLUTIONS FOR CHAPTER 8

In this section, you'll find solutions to the Lab Exercises, Lab Analysis Test, and Key Term Quiz.

Lab Exercise 8.01

At this point you are very much aware that in order to implement a solution provided by Windows 2000, you need to install it. In this lab we installed WINS using the Network and Dial-up Connections Properties. By the end of this lab, you are able to:

■ Install Windows Internet Naming Service

To begin the installation process, perform the following:

Step 1.　Right-click My Network Places on your desktop.

Step 2.　Select Properties from the context menu. The Network and Dial-up Connections window opens.

Step 3.　Click Add Network Components in the lower left corner. This link opens the Windows Components dialog window that shows the Optional Networking Components Windows Wizard.

Step 4.　Choose Network Services as shown in Figure 8-1.

Step 5.　Click Details. This opens the Networking Services window. Make sure the WINS component is checked as shown in Figure 8-2.

Step 6.　Click OK. This brings you back to the previous window.

Step 7.　Click Next to start the wizard. The wizard may prompt you for the Windows 2000 CD if files need to be copied.

Step 8.　Click OK on the summary screen. This window shows the changes that were made.

FIGURE 8-1

Add or remove
Windows 2000
components
through the
Windows Optional
Networking
Components
Wizard

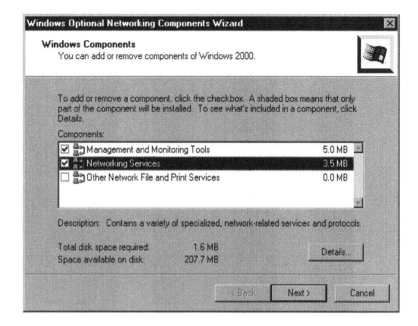

FIGURE 8-2

WINS is one of the
subcomponents that
make up the total
Networking
Components

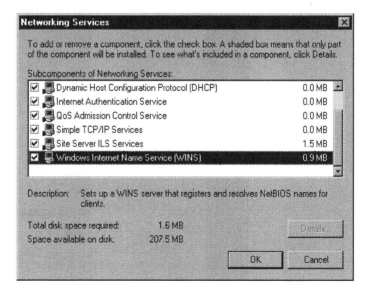

Lab Solution 8.01.1

A number of properties can be configured in the WINS. These properties set the environment in which WINS will operate. A knowledge of setting and modifying these properties ensures proper function of the service. By the end of this lab, you are able to:

- Set static updates
- Set intervals in which records are renewed, deleted, and verified
- Set database verification
- Activate the event log
- Set the request handling number

To reach the properties window and make changes to those properties, perform the following:

Step 1.   Click Start | Programs | Administrative Tools | WINS.

Step 2.   Right-click the server you wish to configure.

Step 3.   Select Properties. The properties window presents you with four tabs.

Step 4.   In the General tab, check the Automatically Update Statistics and set the time interval for every 10 minutes.

Step 5.   In the Intervals tab, set the following rates at which records will be renewed, deleted, and verified as shown in Figure 8-3.

Step 6.   Renew interval: 7 days
Renew interval determines how often the records on WINS get refreshed. More dynamic network environments would require a lower number. The minimum setting for this is 40 minutes and the maximum is 365 days.

Step 7.   Extinction interval: 5 days
Extinction interval is the amount of time a record is marked inactive before it is marked extinct (or tombstoned). The minimum setting for this is 1 hour and the maximum is 365 days.

FIGURE 8-3

Set the automatic refresh rate of WINS server statistics

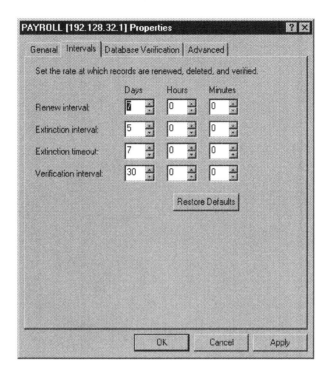

Step 8. Extinction timeout: 7 days

Extinction timeout is the amount of time a record is extinct before it is deleted (scavenged). The minimum setting for this is 24 hours and the maximum is 365 days.

Step 9. Verification interval: 30 days

Verification interval is the periodic integrity check of the information in the database. The minimum setting for this is 24 hours and the maximum is 365 days.

Step 10. In the Database Verification tab, ensure that the consistency of the database is verified every 24 hours. It should begin at 2 hours, and the maximum number of records verified to the originating server is equal to 30,000 as shown in Figure 8-4.

lab
Warning *Don't try this over a slow WAN link.*

Step 11. The Advanced button lets you activate the event log and set the number of WINS requests that the server will accept. Once the limit has been reached, the

FIGURE 8-4

This setting provides automatic database comparisons of replicas to original

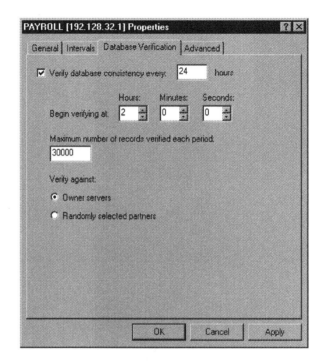

server will return a retry message. Set the level to Medium. The Database Version Number needs no modification. The initial database is given a version of 0. Each subsequent copy of the database will receive a number larger than the previous one.

lab Hint

The server will not send a retry message. The setting here, which becomes available after Enable Burst Handling is checked, is the number of pending registration requests which are allowed to queue before the WINS server switches into "burst handling" mode, whereupon it acknowledges requests without first checking for duplicate names.

Step 12. Click OK to close the window.

Lab Solution 8.02

As in any aspect of networking, redundancy/duplication is an important element to a healthy network, especially when it comes to database information. You want to ensure that if the primary database ever becomes corrupt, you have a backup copy. Or, if you manage a large network with many users and/or encompass a large territory, or spans several states or countries, you have a redundant WINS database to handle the queries. By the end of this of the lab, you are able to:

- Configure WINS replication
- Restrict replication to replication partners only
- Set the Replication Partners Properties
- Enable a push replication to the partner server

To enable WINS replication, perform the following:

Step 1. Click Start | Programs | Administrative Tools | WINS.

Step 2. Select your server in the left side of the window. This will refresh information on the right side of the window.

Step 3. In the right side of the window, right-click Replication Partners and select New Replication Partner.

Step 4. In the WINS server field of the dialog window, enter the name or IP address of another WINS server as shown in Figure 8-5. You can also use the Browse button to search and select the WINS server .

lab
ⓗint

This lab portion requires a second WINS server running on the network. If this is not possible, then you may browse and enter your WINS server. The system will not allow the same database to partner with itself, but you can still perform the steps to become familiar with the screens and prompts.

FIGURE 8-5

This database partner will receive updates from the original source

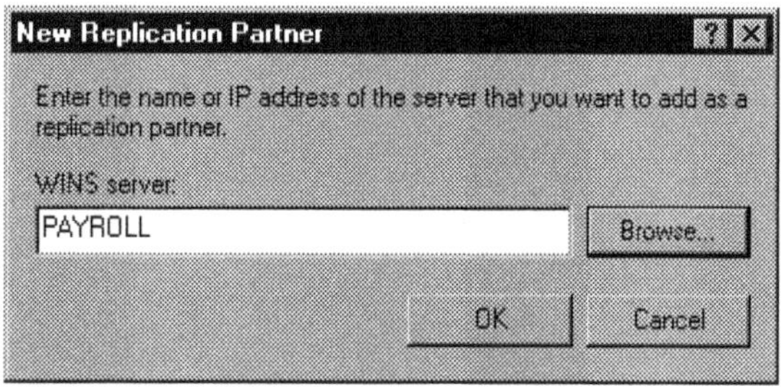

New Replication Partner

Enter the name or IP address of the server that you want to add as a replication partner.

WINS server:
PAYROLL   Browse...

OK   Cancel

Step 5.   Right click Replication Partners on the left side of the window and select Properties. This window has four tabs that need to be configured.

Step 6.   In the General tab restrict replication-to-replication partners only.

Step 7.   Select the Push Replication tab. Here we'll establish replication at service startup and when the address changes. We'll also allow for persistent connections for push replication partners as shown in Figure 8-6.

Step 8.   Once you complete adjusting the settings, click OK to have the settings take effect.

Lab Exercise 8.03

WINS clients register their computer names with a WINS server when they boot up and connect to the network. Clients then query the WINS server to resolve remote

FIGURE 8-6

These settings force replication when the WINS service starts and when client addresses change

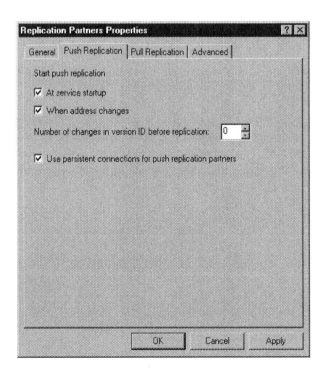

client names. Some of the client-to-WINS server functions include: renewing client names with the WINS database and resolving client names by obtaining IP Address mappings from the WINS database for user names, NetBIOS names, and NetBIOS services. By the of the lab, you will know how to:

■ Configure TCP/IP to use WINS

To configure a WINS client to use a WINS server on your network, perform the following:

Step 1. Open Network and Dial-up Connections.

Step 2. Right-click the network connection you want to configure, and then click Properties.

Step 3. On the General tab select and click Internet Protocol (TCP/IP), and then click Properties.

Step 4. Click Advanced, click the WINS tab, and then click Add.

Step 5. Type the IP address, 192.128.32.1 of the WINS server in the TCP/IP WINS Server window, and then click Add. The IP address is placed in the WINS Addresses List as shown in Figure 8-7.

lab
ⓗint

The use of the Lmhosts file to resolve remote NetBIOS names is enabled by default.

Step 6. Click OK, and all other windows to complete the process.

Lab Exercise 8.04

Ensuring an efficient system requires periodic monitoring of various Windows 2000 components. WINS is no exception. View three of these: Unique Conflicts/Sec, Total Number of Registrations/Sec, and Total Number of Renewals/Sec by using System Monitor. By the end of this lab, you are able to:

■ Monitor Windows 2000 WINS services.

The client
workstation looks
to this WINS
address for
information

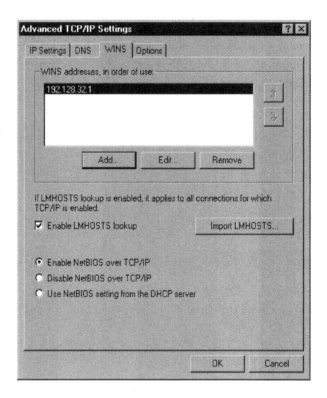

To monitor WINS services perform the following:

Step 1. Click Start | Programs | Administrative Tools | Performance.

Step 2. Select System Monitor from the left side of the split screen in the Performance window.

Step 3. Click the Add (+) icon on the right side of the split screen to create an entry. This opens the Add Counters window.

Step 4. Select the WINS Server in the Performance Object window. A list of counters will display in the window below. Select the following counters as shown in Figure 8-8:

- ■ **Unique Conflicts/Sec** Tracks the rate at which unique client computer registrations or renewals cause conflicts with the database.

- ■ **Total Number of Registrations/Sec** The total of unique single and group registrations per second.

- ■ **Total Number of Renewals/Sec** The total of unique single and group renewals per second.

Step 5. Click Add after each counter that you are going to monitor.

Step 6. Click Close when done. You will now see your counters being graphed.

ANSWERS TO LAB ANALYSIS TEST

1. For all sites to connect to the network, engage WINS on the system. Depending on the network environment, it may be possible to have redundant WINS servers at the central location, or install

FIGURE 8-8

Multiple counters can be selected using the keyboard hotkeys of CTRL and SHIFT

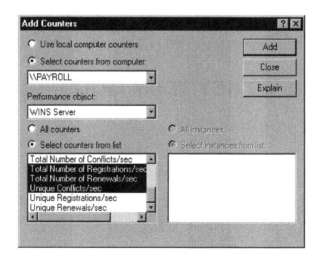

WINS servers at each location. Without additional information we really can't determine that need. In any event, you will still need to configure replication between the servers.

For further information refer to the section on WINS in Chapter 8 of the Windows 2000 Network Administration Study Guide.

2. You will need to configure the WINS servers as replication partners. Once configured they will clone each other based on the parameters you set. To perform this task you would launch the WINS console and expand the WINS server where you want to add the partner. Right-click on the Replication Partners, select New, then select Replication Partners. This can be the name or IP address of the WINS server you wish to add. If you enter a server name that can't be resolved, you will be prompted to enter an IP address instead.

3. Windows 2000 Professional uses H-node (hybrid) for NetBIOS name resolution. This mode favors the WINS for NetBIOS name resolution. If the WINS server is not available, it will attempt to resolve the name by the broadcast method (B-node).

4. Launch the WINS console and select the server in question. Select Server Statistics from the Action menu. If all the queries are returning a Records Not Found, the server has a problem. But, you should check that the number of Records Found is increasing too.

5. The WINS client computer populates the WINS database with client registration data. As the client computer comes online, it registers its name and address with the WINS server. Once registered, the client computer receives what's called "a time to live" for its registration.

ANSWERS TO KEY TERM QUIZ

1. tombstoned

2. WINS

3. B-node

4. pull replication

5. LAN Manager HOSTS (LMHOSTS)

9

Installing, Configuring, Managing, Monitoring, and Troubleshooting IP Routing

LAB EXERCISES

The method that the IP protocol uses to transfer data between networked computers is Internet Protocol (IP) routing. In Windows 2000 IP routing is supported by the Routing and Remote Access Service (RRAS) which was covered in chapter five where remote access features were discussed. This chapter looks at its routing features.

In this chapter we'll work with installing IP routing, implementing routing in Windows 2000 using Routing Information Protocol (RIP) and Open Shortest Path First (OSPF). We'll also configure demand-dial routing and look at managing and monitoring IP routing.

LAB EXERCISE 9.01

Installing IP Routing (Routing and Remote Access)

10 Minutes

Arlene is the network administrator of a small payroll company in the greater Albany, NY area. The network spans two floors and is interconnected using a Windows 2000 Server. Arlene has decided on the need to install and configure IP routing. Setting up IP routing will help move related information between the two interconnected networks. The segments will be class C addresses. What does Arlene need to do to enable IP routing?

Learning Objectives

Arlene's server already has two network cards and a router connected to the network to connect the two segments. Even though Routing and Remote Access Services were installed with Windows 2000 it's still necessary to enable components, such as IP Routing, before the components can be used.

In this lab, you'll perform a basic install of IP Routing using Routing and Remote Access Services Console. These steps assume that Routing and Remote Access Service has already been installed. And, since it's wizard-based it is rather easy to implement. In this lab exercise you will install and set parameters for IP routing. By the end of this lab, you'll be able to:

- Install and Configure IP Routing

Lab Materials and Setup

This lab will require the following items:

- A working computer
- Installed network card
- Routing and Remote Access installed
- Windows 2000 Server software

Getting Down to Business

To begin the installation, perform the following:

Step 1.   Launch Routing and Remote Access console.

Step 2.   Select Configure And Enable Routing And Remote Access on your server. Start the configuration wizard.

Step 3.   Select Network Router on the Common Configuration screen. Setting this option allows different network segments to communicate with each other.

Step 4.   Be sure that TCP/IP is listed in the Remote Client Protocols screen. If you were to communicate with networks that used the Novell's native IPX/SPX protocol, then you would need to add that to your protocol list in Local Area Connection property dialog box. Then the protocol would be available.

Step 5.   Be sure that Yes, All The Required Protocols Are On This List is selected.

Step 6.   Choose Yes on the Demand-Dial Connections window.

Step 7.   Be sure that Automatically is selected on the IP Address Assignment window.

Step 8.   Click Finish to complete the process.

LAB EXERCISE 9.02

Implementing a Statically-Configured Router

15 Minutes

Arlene's next challenge is to set up a static router to connect the two segments. Each segment has about 75 clients, with six application servers in each segment. The segments are connected through the single Windows 2000 Server system that has a network card for each subnet. Arlene has already configured the server to act as a network router in the lab exercise above. She now needs to configure a static router to allow the two segments to communicate. The following information needs to be entered during implementation.

- Destination: 192.128.32.100
- Network mask: 255.255.255.255
- Gateway: 192.128.100.1

Learning Objectives

Internet Protocol (IP) is used to communicate across any set of interconnected IP networks. Static IP routers use routes that are established by an administrator and do not change until the administrator changes them. This type of routing is best suited for small networks and is appropriate for Arlene's payroll network. IP routing is the forwarding of IP traffic from a source host to a destination host through IP routers. At each router, the next hop is determined by matching the destination IP address within the packet with the best route in the routing table. In this lab exercise you'll setup and set parameters for a static router on a small network.

By the end of this lab, you will know how to:

- Enable a static router
- Configure a static router

Lab Material and Setup

This lab will require the following:

- A working computer
- Installed network card
- Routing and Remote Access installed
- Windows 2000 Server software

Getting Down to Business

To enable and configure a Static Router in the Routing and Remote Access Service Console perform the following:

Step 1. Launch Routing and Remote Access console. Select and expand your server.

Step 2. Select and expand the IP Routing container.

Step 3. Choose New Static Route from the menu on the Static Routes container.

Step 4. Enter the following information.

- Interface: Local Area Connection
- Destination: 192.128.32.100
- Network: 255.255.255.255
- Gateway: 192.128.100.1

cross
Reference

The destination IP address is the network ID or an internetwork address for a host route. The network mask determines the IP network ID from a destination IP address, and the subnet mask of 255.255.255.255 indicates a "host router". The gateway address is where the packets will be forwarded. This could either be a hardware address or an internetwork address. For further information refer to the section on Routing in the **Windows 2000 Network Administration Study Guide***.*

Step 5. Click OK to complete the entries.

Step 6. Select the Show IP Routing Table command from the menu on the Static Routes container. Verify the new route information in the dialog box.

Step 7. Click Close to complete the process.

LAB EXERCISE 9.03

Installing and Configuring Routing Information Protocol (RIP)

10 Minutes

You are the systems administrator for Bella Luna Cosmetics Company in Fort Myers, Florida. The network consists of eight segments with Windows 2000 Servers used to connect adjacent segments. Some of these connecting servers are linked to two segments. Routing and Remote Access has been configured to act as a network router on each connecting server. What steps would you take to install and configure RIP on each routing server?

Learning Objectives

Routing Information Protocol (RIP) is by far the most common, easy to configure and deploy, interior routing protocol in use. RIP is what's called a distance vector protocol. This means that it supplies information about the reachable routers on the network, and also provides information about the distances of these networks. These distances are defined by hops, which signifies the number of routers a packet must travel to reach its destination. In this lab exercise you'll install and configure RIP on your Windows 2000 Server. By the end of this lab, you will know how to:

- Install RIP on the Windows 2000 Server
- Configure RIP for the network

Lab Materials and Setup

This lab will require the following:

- A working computer
- Installed network card
- Routing and Remote Access installed
- Windows 2000 Server software

Getting Down to Business

To install and configure RIP perform the following:

Step 1.   Launch Routing and Remote Access console.

Step 2.   Expand IP Routing and right-click General.

Step 3.   Select New Routing Protocol from the menu.

Step 4.   Select RIP Version 2 For Internet Protocol and click OK. You will notice RIP appear under the IP Routing entry. RIP is installed on your Windows 2000 Server.

lab
Hint   *Dynamic routing provides the ability to scale and recover from internetwork errors, rather than static routing, in a medium to very large internetwork.*

Step 5.   Right-click the newly created RIP item and choose New Interface. A dialog box New Interface For RIP Version 2 For Internet Protocol opens.

Step 6.   Select Local Area Connection interface in the window and click OK. This opens the RIP Properties dialog box.

Step 7.   Select RIP Version 1 Broadcast in the Outgoing Packet Protocol window on the General tab. Select RIP Version 1 and 2 in the Incoming Packet Protocol window. Click OK to complete the process.

lab
ⓘint

With RIP version 1, all route announcements are addressed to the IP subnet and a MAC-level broadcast is initiated. Therefore, non-RIP hosts and RIP hosts receive RIP announcements.

LAB EXERCISE 9.04

Installing and Configuring Open Shortest Path First (OSPF)

10 Minutes

You are the systems administrator for Bella Luna Cosmetics Company in Fort Myers, Florida. The company has grown over the past two years. The network now consists of 17 segments with Windows 2000 Servers used to connect adjacent segments. Some of these connecting servers are linked to two segments, and others are now connecting to three or four segments. Routing and Remote Access has been configured to act as a network router on each connecting server. Because of the expanded size of the network, RIP cannot accommodate the internetwork needs. You've decided to install OSPF. What steps would you take to install and configure OSPF on each routing server?

Learning Objectives

Operating as a link-state routing protocol, Open Shortest Path First (OSPF) functions by sending link-state advertisements to all other routers on the same network organization. Link-state protocol means that it creates a routing table of the network, or in other words maps out the network, to calculate the best path of least resistance and congestion. It also includes the state of connection for each router and network segment. In this lab exercise, you'll enable and set parameters for OSPF protocol. By the end of this lab, you will know how to:

- Enable OSPF
- Configure OSPF

Lab Materials and Setup

This lab will require the following:

- A working computer
- Installed network card
- Routing and Remote Access installed
- Windows 2000 Server software

Getting Down to Business

To install and configure OSPF perform the following:

Step 1. Launch Routing and Remote Access console.

Step 2. Expand the console tree. Right-click General under IP Routing.

Step 3. Select New Routing Protocol from the menu.

Step 4. Select Open Shortest Path First (OSPF) from the Routing Protocols window.

Step 5. Click OK to install. OSPF now appears under IP Routing.

Step 6. Right-click on the OSPF and select New Interface from the menu. This opens the New Interface For Open Shortest Path First dialog box.

Step 7. Select Local Area Connection and click OK. The OSPF Properties dialog box opens.

Step 8. On the General tab select the following:

- Enable OSPF for this address
- The area interface ID in Area ID field is set to 0.0.0.0

- Click 1 in Router Priority field
- Click 2 in Cost field
- Set Network Type to Broadcast

Step 9.   Click OK to complete the process.

LAB EXERCISE 9.05

Implementing Demand-Dial Routing

10 Minutes

The law office of Laythem, Ooutt, and Lavender Inc. has two large offices, one in New York and the other in Los Angeles. A Virtual Private Networking (VPN) link is used to communicate and transfer data between the two locations. However, the VPN connection periodically goes offline due to Internet congestion or ISP issues. Management has asked you, the network engineer, to put a backup plan in place that will provide an alternate connection when these VPN failures occur. Management also wants you to keep costs in mind when determining a solution.

Learning Objectives

The first solution that would come to mind would be a dedicated line between the two sites. But once cost enters the picture, this type of solution for a small network exits the picture as quickly as it entered. The low-cost plan would be to implement an on-demand telephone route option.

Demand-Dial Routing is a routing technique that allows a user to utilize existing telephone lines as a way to connect to a destination. The connection only becomes active when data is sent to the remote site. When no data has been sent over the link for a specified amount of time, the link is disconnected.

This connection between sites is only established when a specific type of traffic initiates the call, or when a backup link is needed for redundancy or load sharing.

Demand-Dial Routing is also used in order to save on the costs of a dedicated WAN line for organizations that do not need permanent, continuous, connection.

In this lab exercise, you'll enable and configure Demand-Dial Routing on a Windows 2000 Server. By the end of this lab, you will know how to:

- Add Demand-Dial Routing using Routing and Remote Access Console
- Set the Connection Type
- Set protocols to be routed
- Enter login information for remote router

Lab Materials and Setup

This lab will require the following:

- A working computer
- Installed network card
- Installed modem
- Routing and Remote Access installed
- Windows 2000 Server software

Getting Down to Business

To implement Demand-Dial Routing perform the following:

Step 1.   Launch Routing and Remote Access console.

Step 2.   Expand the console tree and right-click the server. Select Properties from the menu. The *servername* (local) Properties dialog box opens.

Step 3.   Select LAN And Demand-Dial Routing on the General tab. Return to the RRAS console.

Step 4.   Right-click Routing Interfaces and select New Demand-Dial Interface from the menu. The Demand-Dial Interface wizard will appear.

Step 5. In the Interface Name dialog box enter Dialup Router .

Step 6. In the Connection Type dialog box, select Connect Using a Modem, ISDN Adapter, or Other Physical Device.

Step 7. The next window that appears is the Select A Device dialog box. The modem connected to the server will appear on the list. Select the serial device you wish to use as a connection interface.

Step 8. In the Phone Number dialog box, enter the phone number of the answering router.

Step 9. In the Protocols and Security dialog box select the protocols you need to route over this connection. You need to select Route IP Packets On This Interface.

Step 10. In the Dial Out Credentials dialog box enter the following information:

- User name: JTosano
- Domain: Southernbell
- Password: password
- Confirm password: password

This information will allow you to connect to the answering router.

lab
①int
The remote router will have to be configured with a user account and password corresponding to the ones used above, and have remote access permissions which will allow the connection to take place.

Step 11. Click Finish to complete the process.

LAB EXERCISE 9.06

Monitoring IP Routing Protocols

5 Minutes

Mondays are always busy at the support desk where twelve people handle all types of calls. You receive a call from Al, a user who is trying to transfer information from his computer to another user's computer. You check into the issue and determine that each computer is on a different segment of the network. Configurations on each computer are fine, and you are able to ping to their IP address. You tell Al that you need to investigate further. What tool would you use?

Learning Objectives

The appropriate tool for this scenario is Network Monitor. It allows you to view and capture network traffic. It's also the tool that can help you diagnose problems between computers that cannot communicate or even when a computer has trouble operating within a network environment. This may deal with resolving names, or having a routing problem.

In this lab exercise, we're concerned with capturing network traffic for computers that cannot communicate. By the end of this lab, you will know how to:

- Launch Network Monitor
- View Network Monitor statistics

Lab Materials and Setup

This lab will require the following:

- A working computer
- Installed network card
- Windows 2000 Server software

Getting Down to Business

To capture and monitor IP Routing Protocols perform the following:

Step 1.   Launch Network Monitor.

Step 2.   In the Select A Network screen expand Local Computer and select the network to monitor. Click OK.

Step 3.   Initiate a capture session to begin the benchmark process.

LAB ANALYSIS TEST

1. Arnold, a LAN administrator at Minute-Man Security, has just completed a default Windows 2000 Server installation on a computer with two network cards. During such an installation, which dynamic routing protocols are installed by default?

   _____

   _____

2. Jill is a network administrator for a Windows 2000 network. She is using autostatic updates. What must she do the first time you connect to a remote router?

   _____

   _____

3. Arthur and Carrie discuss the advantages of OSPF rather than RIP version 2 for their company's Windows 2000 network. What advantages does OSPF have over RIP version 2?

   _____

   _____

4. You have configured a Demand-Dial Routing connection between your corporate office in Chicago, Illinois and your regional office in Phoenix, Arizona. You have configured RIP as the routing protocol and set it up as a persistent connection. However, when you try to contact a host workstation from the corporate office to the regional office, you cannot reach it. You retrace your configuration steps and everything seems fine. What could the problem be?

   _____

   _____

5. You've replaced your existing Novell server router with a Windows 2000 Server configured as a router. Three segments have been configured and connected to the server each having a Class C address associated with it. You've configured the related route commands to add the network entries to the static routing table. The subnet mask is set to 255.255.255.0 with no default gateway configured for the router. What happens to a packet that arrives for a route that hasn't been configured on the router?

   _____

   _____

KEY TERM QUIZ

Use the following vocabulary terms to complete the sentences below. Not all of the terms will be used.

> Open Shortest Path First (OSPF)
>
> Split horizon
>
> IP routing
>
> Routing Internet Protocol (RIP)
>
> Dynamic routing
>
> Exterior Gateway Protocol (EGP)
>
> Interior Gateway Protocol (IGP)
>
> Border Gateway Protocol (BGP)
>
> distance vector protocol
>
> static route

1. _____ allows routers to learn available routes automatically. Typical protocols include RIP, OSPF, and BGP.

2. _____ is the original outside protocol used to exchange routing information between different and unassociated networks.

3. A protocol used by dynamic routers, _____ is used to share the dynamic routing tables.

4. This particular protocol, _____, has a maximum path length of 15 hops. If the data packet has to travel beyond the 15 hops, then RIP considers the destination unreachable.

5. _____ is the original exterior protocol used to exchange routing information between unique networks.

LAB WRAP-UP

In this lab chapter we focused mainly on routing. We covered the fundamentals of routing and enabled distance-vector routing (RIP) and link-state routing (OSPF). We looked at implementing both of these types of IP routing, Routing Information Protocol and Open Shortest Path First protocol. Both of these protocols serve certain network and internetwork sizes, from small to large. We also configured Demand-Dial Routing that provides a site for connecting remote locations or for providing a backup method of connecting two sites. Lastly, we looked at managing and monitoring IP routing through the use of the Network Monitor utility.

LAB SOLUTIONS FOR CHAPTER 9

Lab Solution 9.01

First, be sure that Routing and Remote Access Service has been installed on your server. And, since IP Routing is wizard-based, it is rather easy to implement. In this lab exercise you will install and set parameters for IP routing. By the end of this lab, you'll be able to:

- Install and Configure IP Routing

To begin the installation, perform the following:

Step 1. Click Start | Programs | Administrative Tools | Routing and Remote Access.

Step 2. Right-click the computer name and select Configure And Enable Routing And Remote Access as seen in Figure 9-1. Click Next on the Welcome screen.

Step 3. Select the Network Router option on the Common Configuration screen as seen in Figure 9-2. Click Next.

FIGURE 9-1

This will start the RRAS server setup

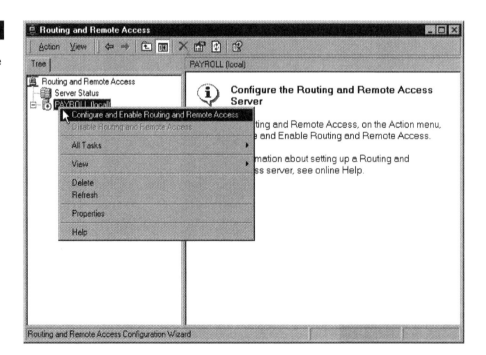

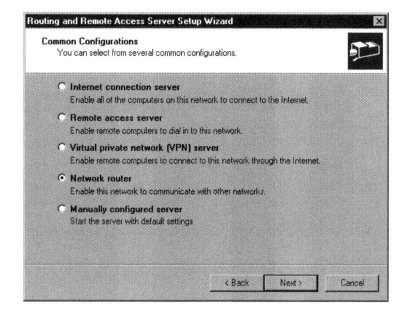

FIGURE 9-2

Customize the
wizard to
configure the
server for a
specific task

Step 4.   Be sure that TCP/IP is listed in the Remote Client Protocols screen.

Step 5.   Be sure that Yes, All The Required Protocols Are On This List is selected.
Click Next.

Step 6.   Choose Yes on the Demand-Dial Connections window.

Step 7.   Be sure that Automatically is selected on the IP Address Assignment window.
Click Next.

Step 8.   Click Finish to complete the process.

Lab Solution 9.02

Static IP routers use tables that are created and maintained by an administrator.
These tables do not change until the administrator changes them. Use of static IP
routers on large networks would create a large amount of maintenance overhead.
In this lab exercise you'll setup and set parameters for a static router on a small network.

By the end of this lab, you will be able to:

- Enable a static router
- Configure a static router

To enable and configure a Static Router in the Routing and Remote Access Service Console perform the following:

Step 1. Click Start | Programs | Administrative Tools | Routing and Remote Access.

Step 2. Select and expand the server you wish to configure on the left pane of the window.

Step 3. Select and expand the IP Routing container under the server.

Step 4. Right-click the Static Routes container, and choose New Static Route from the menu. A Static Route dialog box appears as in Figure 9-3.

Step 5. From the Interface pull-down list, select the interface you want to use.

FIGURE 9-3

Set the destination parameters for each field

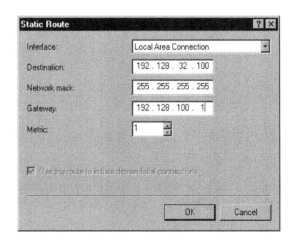

Step 6.   Enter the destination IP address for the route network: 192.128.32.100. Enter the corresponding network mask: 255.255.255.0. Enter the Gateway's IP address: 192.128.100.1.

Step 7.   Enter the RRAS server's IP address in the Gateway field.

Step 8.   Click OK to complete the entry.

Step 9.   Right-click the Static Routes container in the left window pane, and select the Show IP Routing Table command from the menu.

Step 10.   Verify the new route information in the dialog box as shown in Figure 9-4.

Step 11.   Click Close to complete the process.

FIGURE 9-4

This is a snapshot of the routing table

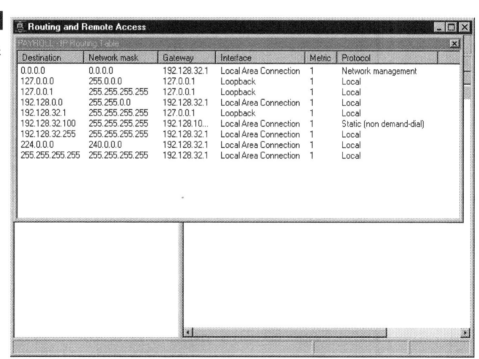

Lab Solution 9.03

The way RIP works is rather simple. Every 30 second interval a RIP-enabled router will broadcast its routing table to the network. A receiving router that is RIP-enabled will add the information to its table. In this lab exercise you will install and configure RIP on our Windows 2000 Server. By the end of this lab, you'll be able to:

- Install RIP on the Windows 2000 Server
- Configure RIP for the network

To install and configure RIP perform the following:

Step 1. Click Start | Programs | Administrative Tools | Routing and Remote Access.

Step 2. Expand the list under IP Routing in the left windowpane and right-click General.

Step 3. Select New Routing Protocol from the menu. This opens the New Routing Protocol dialog box.

Step 4. Select RIP Version 2 For Internet Protocol and click OK. You will notice that RIP appears under the IP Routing entry as shown in Figure 9-5. RIP is installed on your Windows 2000 Server.

lab
ⓗint

Dynamic routing provides the ability to scale and recover from internetwork errors, rather than static routing, in a medium to very large internetwork.

Step 5. Right-click the newly created RIP item under IP Routing in the left windowpane and choose New Interface. A dialog box New Interface For RIP Version 2 For Internet Protocol opens.

Step 6. Select Local Area Connection interface in the window and click OK. This opens the RIP Properties dialog box.

FIGURE 9-5

Add RIP version 2
Internet Protocol
from the New
Router Protocol
window

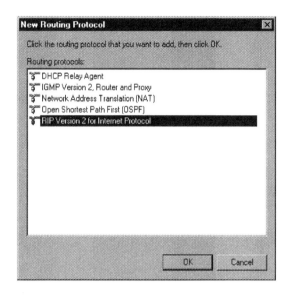

Step 7.   Select RIP Version 1 Broadcast in the Outgoing Packet Protocol window on the General tab. Select RIP Version 1 And 2 in the Incoming Packet Protocol window. Click OK to complete the process.

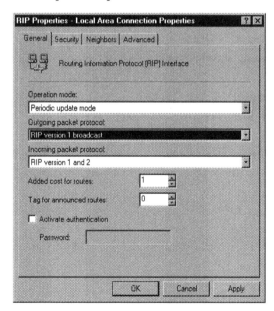

Lab Solution 9.04

The best thing going for OSPF is that it is efficient. It requires little overhead, even if it's implemented in a large inter-connected network. Unlike RIP, OSPF does not exchange entire routing table entries. Instead, a map of the internetwork is maintained by each OSPF router. In this lab exercise, you'll enable and set parameters for OSPF protocol. By the end of this lab, you will know how to:

- Enable OSPF
- Configure OSPF

To setup and enable OSPF perform the following:

Step 1. Click Start | Programs | Administrative Tools | Routing and Remote Access.

Step 2. In the left window pane expand the console tree. Right-click General under IP Routing.

Step 3. Select New Routing Protocol from the menu. This opens the New Routing Protocol dialog box.

Step 4. Select Open Shortest Path First (OSPF) from the Routing Protocols window as shown in Figure 9-6.

Step 5. Click OK to install. OSPF now appears under IP Routing in the left window pane.

Step 6. Right-click on the OSPF and select New Interface from the menu. This opens the New Interface For Open Shortest Path First dialog box.

Step 7. Select Local Area Connection and click OK. The OSPF Properties dialog box opens.

Add OSPF from
the New Router
Protocol window

New Routing Protocol

Click the routing protocol that you want to add, then click OK.

Routing protocols:

DHCP Relay Agent
IGMP Version 2, Router and Proxy
Network Address Translation (NAT)
Open Shortest Path First (OSPF)

OK   Cancel

Step 8.   On the General tab select the following:

- enable OSPF for this address
- the area interface ID in Area ID field is set to 0.0.0.0
- click 1 in Router Priority field
- click 2 in Cost field
- set Network Type to Broadcast

Step 9.   Click OK to complete the process.

Lab Solution 9.05

Demand-Dial Routing is a routing technique that allows a user to utilize existing
telephone lines as a way to connect to a destination.

Demand-Dial Routing is primarily used for low-traffic network environments.
This dial-up connection is activated when data is transmitted to or received from a
distant server.

Demand-Dial Routing is also used in order to save on the costs of a dedicated
WAN line for organizations that do not need permanent, continuous, connection.

In this lab exercise, you'll enable and configure Demand-Dial Routing on a Windows 2000 Server. By the end of this lab, you will be able to:

- Add Demand-Dial Routing using Routing and Remote Access Console
- Set the Connection Type
- Set protocols to be routed
- Enter login information for remote router

To enable and configure Demand-Dial Routing perform the following:

Step 1. Click Start | Programs | Administrative Tools | Routing and Remote Access.

Step 2. In the left windowpane expand the console tree and right-click the server. Select Properties from the menu. The *servername* (local) Properties dialog box opens.

Step 3. Select LAN and Demand-Dial Routing on the General tab as shown in Figure 9-7. Click OK to return to the RRAS console.

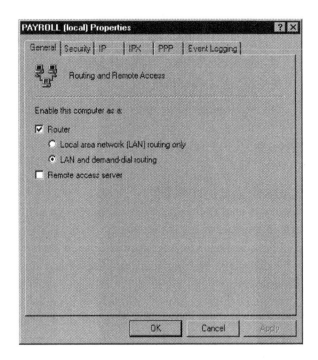

FIGURE 9-7

The router is set to be either a dedicated LAN router, and/or a demand-dial route

Step 4.   Right-click Routing Interfaces and select New Demand-Dial Interface from the menu. The Demand-Dial Interface wizard will appear.

Step 5.   Click Next to proceed. In the Interface Name dialog box enter the Interface name. Click Next to continue.

Step 6.   The Connection Type dialog box appears. Select Connect Using a Modem, ISDN Adapter, or Other Physical Device. Click Next to continue.

Step 7.   The next window that appears is the Select A Device dialog box. The modem connected to the server will appear on the list. Select the serial device you wish to use as a connection interface and click Next.

Step 8.   The Phone Number dialog box appears. Enter the phone number of the answering router. Click Next to continue.

Step 9.   The Protocols And Security dialog box appears. Here you can select the protocols you need to route over this connection. You need to select Route IP Packets On This Interface as shown in Figure 9-8. Click Next to continue.

FIGURE 9-8

Select the routed protocols and security for demand-dial connection

Step 10. The Dial Out Credentials dialog box appears. Enter the following information:

- User Name: JToscano
- Domain: Southernbell
- Password: password
- Confirm password: password

This information as shown in Figure 9-9 will allow you to connect to the answering router. Click Next to continue.

Step 11. Click Finish to complete the process.

Lab Solution 9.06

Once again, Network Monitor is the tool that can help you diagnose problems between computers that cannot communicate or even when a computer has trouble operating within a network environment.

FIGURE 9-9

The login credentials are necessary to connect to a remote router

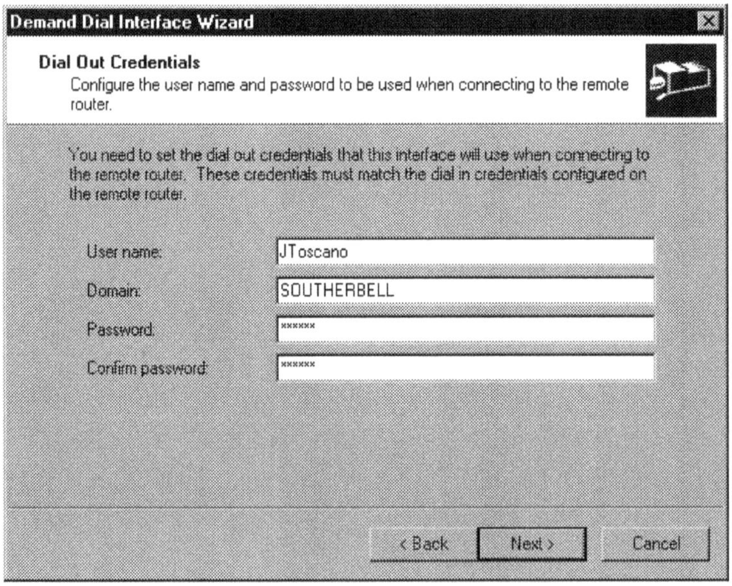

In this lab exercise, your focus is on capturing network traffic for computers that cannot communicate. By the end of this lab, you will be able to:

- Launch Network Monitor
- View Network Monitor statistics

To capture and monitor network traffic perform the following:

Step 1.　Click Start | Programs | Administrative Tools | Network Monitor.

Step 2.　The Select A Network screen will open. Expand Local Computer and select the network to monitor.

Step 3.　Click Capture from the Menu Bar. Select Start. This actives the monitoring process as shown in Figure 9-10.

FIGURE 9-10

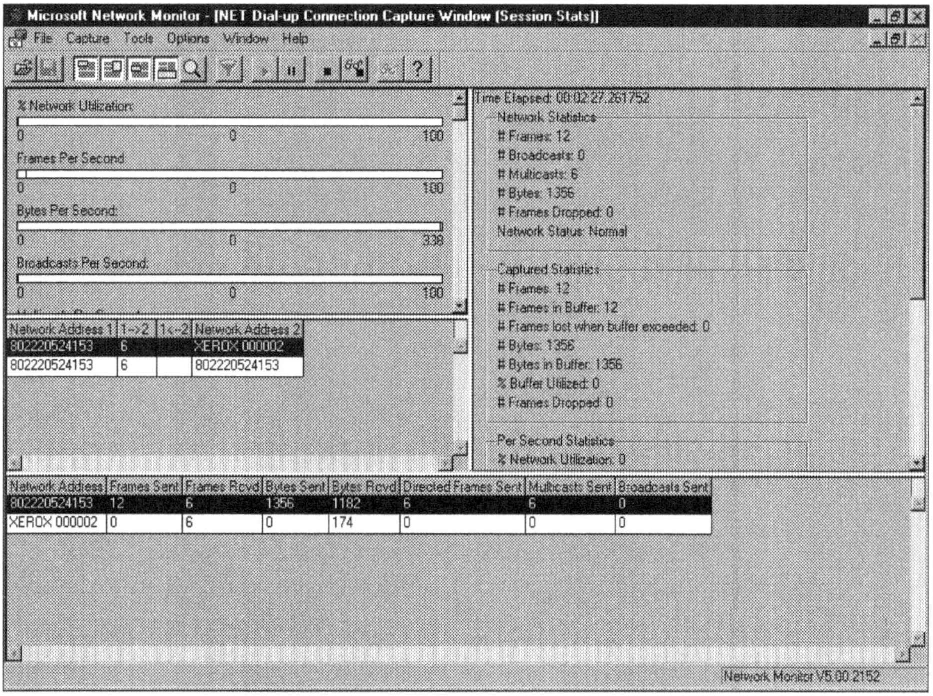

Network Monitor can be configured to capture network traffic

Step 4. One of the screens within Network Monitor tracks IP Router statistics.

ANSWERS TO LAB ANALYSIS TEST

I. There are two routing protocols that are installed on the server, RIP and OSPF. RIP, which is distance-vector protocol, specifies how routers exchange routing table information. RIP makes some basic design choices. Each node in the network keeps a routing table. This routing table contains entries, limited to 15, for all the reachable nodes in the network. OSPF is a link-state protocol where each router actively tests the status of its link to each of its neighbors, sends this information to its other neighbors, and so on. In a link-state protocol each router takes this link-state information and builds a complete routing table.

cross
Reference *For more information refer to the section on Routing Protocols in Chapter 9 of the* **Windows 2000 Network Administration Study Guide.**

2. When initializing a demand-dial connection, autostatic updates do not occur automatically. They need to be manually set or placed on a schedule to update the routes. After the routes have been sent, the two connecting routers exchange updates of routing information only after a manual request is made or a scheduled request occurs. So, the first time a connection is made, an autostatic update has to be manually set to configure the proper routes to the destination network.

3. Open Shortest Path First (OSPF) is becoming the standard in Windows 2000 routed networks. It is slowly replacing the older RIP version 2. There are many advantages to OSPF that makes it the favored protocol. The biggest advantage is efficiency. It requires very little overhead. You can use multicast rather than broadcast, and you can have protection from rogue routers with an encrypted password. Routing tables are smaller, which results in faster convergence. IT can support routing paths greater than 15 routers. And, OSPF routes are loop-free.

cross
Reference *For more information refer to the section on OSPF in Chapter 9 of the* **Windows 2000 Network Administration Study Guide.**

4. In this particular situation, an autostatic update has not occurred. Therefore, no routing information is available to let the source location reach the destination location. When a demand-dial connection is initialized, the autostatic updates do not occur automatically. You have to either manually request the updates, or set up the request on a schedule.

5. If a default gateway is not configured, the router drops the packet and sends an Internet Control Message Protocol (ICMP) message back to the source location indicating that the destination location is unreachable.

ANSWERS TO KEY TERM QUIZ

1. dynamic routing

2. EGP

3. RIP

4. distance vector protocol

5. EGP

MICROSOFT CERTIFIED SYSTEMS ENGINEER

10

Installing, Configuring, and Troubleshooting NAT

LAB EXERCISES

I f a small office needs to provide simultaneous access to users, each user would need a valid IP address. This can get costly. A way to share one Internet access IP address is to implement Internet Connection Sharing (ICS), a service that is easy to configure and manage. The protocol that provides the vehicle for sharing a single connection is Network Address Translation. These private addresses are assigned internally and then translate between the private address and the public address. The public address is used as a gateway out to the Internet.

In this chapter we look at ICS and NAT and the services they provide. After installing and configuring both ICS and NAT, we look at how to logically troubleshoot NAT services.

LAB EXERCISE 10.01

Exploring Internet Connection Sharing (ICS) and Network Address Translation (NAT)

15 Minutes

You are the network administrator for Soar High Travel Agency. It's a small network running on a Windows 2000 system. Your manager is planning on getting Internet access to the agents in the office. He recently went to a Travel Agents trade show where one of the vendor booths had a presentation about Small Office Home Office (SOHO) networking. At the presentation, the presenter talked about Network Address Translation and Internet Connection Sharing. Your manager really didn't understand so he has asked you to explain the difference between NAT protocols and the ICS services in a short report by the end of the week.

Learning Objectives

In this lab you'll identify and explain the purpose of NAT and ICS and the features that allow small offices to connect to the Internet. By the end of this lab, you'll be able to:

■ Understand and explain how ICS allows an easy connection to the Internet

■ Understand and explain how NAT helps share a single connection to the Internet

Lab Materials and Setup

This lab will require the following items:

- Pencil and paper
- Windows 2000 Server

Getting Down to Business

Address each service separately and list their features and benefits:

Step 1. In the space below, briefly list the benefits that ICS provides in allowing users on a small network to connect to the Internet.

_____

_____

Step 2. In the space below, briefly list the benefits that NAT provides in allowing users to connect to the Internet using a single IP address.

_____

_____

LAB EXERCISE 10.02

Installing and Configuring Internet Connection Sharing (ICS)

You are the system administrator for We'll-Take-You-There Guide Service in the New Hampshire White Mountains. You have a Windows 2000 Server connected to the Internet and four computers connected on the network. You need to install ICS on the server in order to connect to the Internet through the server. How would you enable this feature?

Learning Objectives

In this lab exercise you will enable ICS on each computer connected on the network. By the end of this lab, you will be able to:

- Install ICS on a client computer
- Configure ICS on a client computer

Lab Materials and Setup

This lab will require the following:

- A working computer
- Installed network card
- Window 2000 Professional software

Getting Down to Business

To install and configure Internet Connection Sharing (ICS) on a Windows 2000 Server, perform the following:

Step 1.   Open the Network and Dial-up Connections window.

Step 2.   Access the Connection Properties dialog box of your Internet Connection icon.

Step 3.   Select Enable Internet Connection Sharing For This Connection in the Sharing tab.

Step 4.   Click OK to complete the installation.

LAB EXERCISE 10.03

Installing and Configuring Network Address Sharing (NAT)

15 Minutes

You are the network administrator for the museum's ticket reservation service. You've just installed a Windows 2000 Server, on a network with ten computers, to connect the network to the Internet. The museum was able to purchase only one IP address. What is the most cost-effective item or component to add to the server to let the users simultaneously connect to the Internet.

Learning Objectives

In this lab exercise you'll install and configure NAT on your Windows 2000 Server. By the end of this lab, you will know how to:

- Install NAT on the Windows 2000 Server
- Configure NAT for the network

Lab Materials and Setup

This lab will require the following:

- A working computer
- Installed network card
- Routing and Remote Access Server
- Windows 2000 Server software

Getting Down to Business

To perform the installation of NAT on the Windows 2000 Server, perform the following:

Step 1. Launch Routing and Remote Access Console.

Step 2. Expand the IP Routing icon and right-click on General. Select New Routing Protocol.

Step 3. Select Network Address Translation and click OK.

Step 4. Right-click the newly created Network Address Translation icon and select Properties. In the General tab select Log Errors And Warnings, if it's not already selected.

Step 5. Select the Address Assignment tab. Select Automatically Assign IP Address By Using DHCP. This tab lets you configure the private IP addresses and configure the DHCP service used in conjunction with NAT.

- Verify the IP address: 192.168.0.0
- Verify the Mask: 255.255.255.0

Step 6. Click OK to complete the process and return to the RRAS console.

Now we need to configure the NAT interface.

Step 7. Right-click the NAT icon again and select New Interface.

Step 8. Select Remote Router as the interface to be used as the LAN interface and click OK.

Step 9. The dialog box for that connection opens. You will set this interface as an external connection. Therefore, select Public Connection To The Internet.

Step 10. Click OK to complete this process.

Repeat the above steps for the Private Connection to the Internet.

LAB EXERCISE 10.04

Troubleshooting Techniques for NAT

15 Minutes

As a LAN administrator, you periodically have to attend conferences and vendor shows that apply to networking, software, and hardware issues and innovations. You've just completed a NAT install and configuration on your Windows 2000 Server. You want to make sure that in your absence, your boss can easily troubleshoot any issues that may arise with NAT. You need to put together a list of general steps that he can follow if he needs to resolve a NAT issue.

Learning Objectives

In this lab you'll identify the steps to take to help troubleshoot NAT. By the end of this lab, you will know how to:

■ List and explain troubleshooting steps when resolving problems with NAT

Lab Materials and Setup

For this lab exercise, you'll need:

■ Pencil and paper
■ Windows 2000 Server

Getting Down to Business

Since you are preparing instructions for someone else to follow, the steps must be compiled in the order you would use them.

Step 1 You need to create a logical plan to help solve any potential problem with NAT. In the space, put together a game plan that you would follow to resolve issues specific to NAT.

LAB ANALYSIS TEST

1. As the network administrator of a small frozen food delivery company, you are asked to connect to the Internet for the first time. The company has only 12 employees, and you don't possess a lot of experience with Windows 2000 or routing. What service should you install to ensure that the employees could successfully connect to the Internet?

   _____

   _____

2. Your surgical supply company, A Cut Above, with a 100-user network, has had you install a Windows 2000 Server to connect the network to the Internet. As the LAN administrator, you need to resolve a problem. None of your users are able to connect to the Internet even though the server does connect. What do you think may be the problem?

   _____

   _____

3. You're the administrator of the Up-Market Investment Agency's Windows 2000 Server, and you're considering setting up NAT. What benefit would NAT provide?

   _____

   _____

4. Small Wonders Toy Co. has recently installed several Windows 2000 Server systems and upgraded some clients to Windows 2000 Professional. Other computers on the system include Windows NT and Windows 98. The network needs Internet access, so the company has leased a dedicated 256 MB fiber optic connection. Which additional cost-effective services need to be enabled on a Windows 2000 Server to allow users to connect to the Internet?

   _____

   _____

5. You are the junior engineer for the Double-Vision Marketing Co. and you've installed and configured NAT on your Windows 2000 Server. What's the easiest way to monitor the connection usage?

   _____

   _____

KEY TERM QUIZ

Use the following vocabulary terms to complete the sentences below. Not all of the terms will be used.

Internet Connection Sharing

Network Address Translation

Request For Comments

registered IP address

private IP address

Internet Service Provider

Domain Name System

User Datagram Protocol (UDP)

Internet Key Exchange

Preshared Keys

1. _____ is a connectionless protocol that's used to define a resource on a Windows 2000 Server and end-to-end data transmission.

2. The Internet Engineering Task Force specifies the details for protocols through the use of documents named _____.

3. A Windows 2000 service, _____, is used to allow a small office to share a dial-up Internet connection.

4. _____ is an IP address range reserved for in-house, non-internet connected, networks. These are private address ranges within Classes A, B, and C.

5. An Internet standard, _____, allows a Windows 2000 Server to use a set of IP addresses on an internal network and a set of IP addresses on an external network.

LAB WRAP-UP

In this chapter we looked at ICS and NAT and the services they provide. We compared the two components and the features they offer. We installed and configured Internet Connection Sharing (ICS) on a client computer and a server. We installed and configured Network Address Translation (NAT) on a Windows 2000 Server. Lastly we looked at troubleshooting techniques for NAT and how to logically problem-solve the NAT service.

LAB SOLUTIONS FOR CHAPTER 10

Lab Solution 10.01

Your manager wants to get Internet access to the agents in the office. He heard about the features of Network Address Translation and Internet Connection Sharing. Because he didn't understand the presentation, he's asked you to explain the difference between NAT protocols and the ICS services in a short report by the end of the week.

In this lab you identify and explain the purpose of NAT and ICS and the features that allow small offices to connect to the Internet. By the end of this lab, you will know how to:

- Explain how ICS allows an easy connection to the Internet
- Explain how NAT helps share a single connection to the Internet

Step 1.   Internet Connection Sharing has the following benefits:

- Easiest to implement
- Installable on any network, preferably on small networks
- Also includes Demand-Dial Routing
- Configurable on a Windows 2000 Professional or Server computer
- Combines AutoDHCP and DNS proxy

Step 2.   Network Address Translation has the following benefits:

- Installed using Routing and Remote Access utility
- Allows sharing of one leased IP address for concurrent Internet connection
- Affords security by hiding the internal structure of the network
- Reduced cost through the use of private IP addresses using one leased IP address
- Provides scalability

Lab Solution 10.02

As system administrator for We'll-Take-You-There Guide Service in the New Hampshire White Mountains your task is to install ICS on the Windows 2000 Server in order to connect to the Internet through the server.

In this lab exercise you'll enable ICS on the server providing Internet service connected on the network. By the end of this lab, you will know how to:

- Install ICS on a Windows 2000 Server
- Configure ICS on a Windows 2000 Server

To install and configure Internet Connection Sharing on a client computer perform the following:

Step 1.   Right-click on My Network Places icon and select Properties to open the Network and Dial-up Connections window.

Step 2.   Right-click the dial-up connection icon that represents your Internet connection and select Properties. The Connection Properties dialog box opens.

Step 3.   Click the Sharing tab. Select the Enable Internet Connection Sharing For This Connection option as shown in Figure 10-1.

lab
ⓘint   *Notice that the Enable On Demand dialing option is selected by default.*

Step 4.   Click OK. A warning appears stating that the IP address of the adaptor will change if you continue as shown in Figure 10-2. Click Yes to complete the installation.

Lab Solution 10.03

In this scenario you've just installed a Windows 2000 Server on a network with ten computers to connect the network to the Internet. Because the museum was able to purchase only one IP address to connect to the Internet, you need to add NAT.

In this lab exercise you will install and configure NAT on your Windows 2000 Server. By the end of this lab, you'll be able to:

- Install NAT on the Windows 2000 Server
- Configure NAT for the network

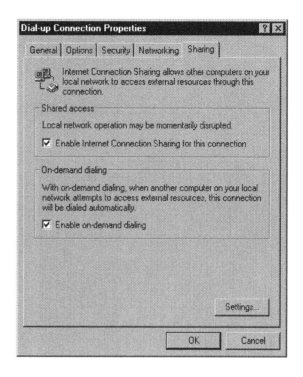

Step 1.   Click Start | Programs | Administrative Tools | Routing and Remote
Access Console.

Step 2.   Expand the IP Routing icon in the left window pane and right-click
on General.

Step 3.   Select New Routing Protocol to open the dialog box shown in Figure 10-3.

Step 4.   Select Network Address Translation, as shown in Figure 10-3, and click
OK. The Network Address Translation icon will show as an icon under IP Routing.

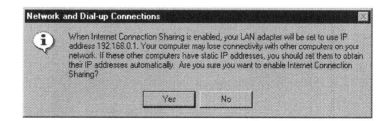

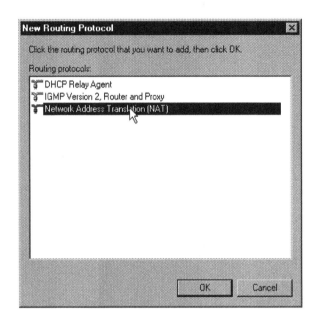

Step 5. Right-click the newly created Network Address Translation icon and select Properties. In the General tab select Log Errors And Warnings, if it's not already selected as shown in Figure 10-4.

lab
Warning   *It's important to periodically check the Event Viewer for any errors or warnings that pertain to NAT.*

Step 6. Select the Address Assignment tab. Select Automatically Assign IP Address By Using DHCP as shown in Figure 10-5. This tab lets you configure the private IP addresses and configure the DHCP service used in conjunction with NAT.

■ Verify the IP address: 192.168.0.0
■ Verify the Mask: 255.255.255.0

Step 7. Click OK to complete the process and return to the RRAS console. Now we need to configure the NAT interface.

Step 8. Right-click the NAT icon again and select New Interface. The New Interface For Nat dialog box opens.

FIGURE 10-4

Setting event
logging for errors
and warnings is a
good idea for a
smaller network

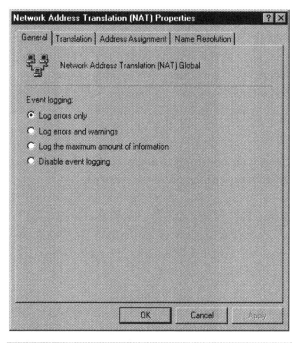

FIGURE 10-5

The Address
Assignment tab
lets you set the
DHCP service for
the NAT protocol

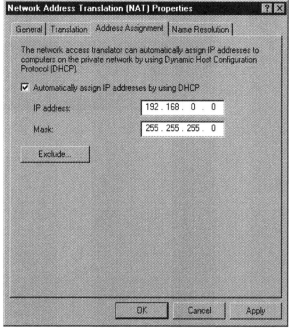

Step 9. Select Remote Router as the interface to be used as the LAN interface and click OK as shown in Figure 10-6.

Step 10. The dialog box for that connection opens. You will set this interface as an external connection. Therefore, select Public Interface Connected To The Internet. Also select Translate TCP/UDP Headers. Selecting this option designates this computer as the interface of data transmission. Both are shown in Figure 10-7.

lab

ⓗint

Since you are using a single public IP address allocated by your ISP, no other IP address configuration is needed.

Step 11. Click OK to complete this process.

The above steps have configured NAT as an external connection to the internet using the assigned IP address. The following steps will configure another interface for the local connection.

Step 12. Right-click NAT again and select New Interface. The New Interface For NAT dialog box opens.

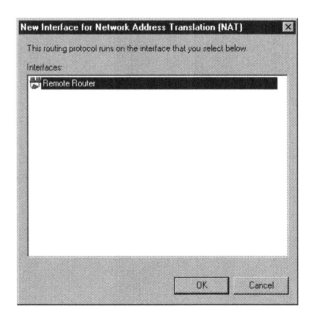

Select the new interface for the NAT routing protocol

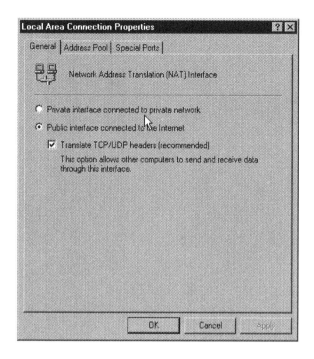

Step 13.   Select Local Area Connection as the interface to be used as the LAN interface and click OK as shown in Figure 10-8.

Step 14.   The dialog box for that connection opens. You will set this interface as an internal connection. Therefore, select Private Interface Connected To The Private Network as shown in Figure 10-9.

Step 11.   Click OK to complete this process.

Lab Solution 10.04

Your task in this scenario is to put together a list of general steps that your boss can follow if he needs to resolve a NAT issue. In this lab you'll identify the steps to take to help troubleshoot NAT. By the end of this lab, you will be able to:

■   List and explain troubleshooting steps when resolving problems with NAT

FIGURE 10-8

Select the routing
protocol for the
internal network

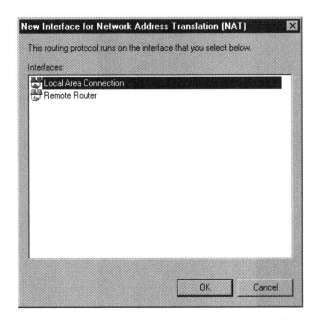

FIGURE 10-9

This window
identifies the
NAT interface as
connected to a
private network

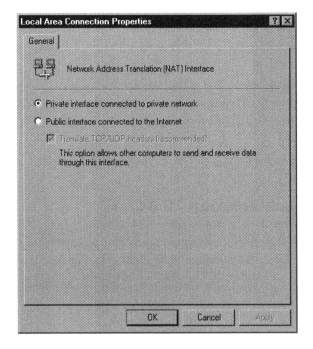

Step 1. Perform an Internet connection check after each of the following steps. Once the problem is resolved, you can stop the troubleshooting process.

- The first step to take is to check network connections using the ping, pingpath, or tracert commands
- Check that at least the public and private interfaces for NAT are defined
- Stop and restart the Routing and Remote Access service
- Reboot the Routing and Remote Access host system
- Delete and re-create NAT interfaces
- Remove and reinstall the NAT routing protocol

ANSWERS TO LAB ANALYSIS TEST

1. The perfect solution for a small company is to implement Internet Connection Sharing, which also bundles the services necessary to make the connection work.

2. You need to install NAT for the connection to work. NAT allows the company to use private addresses on its internal network and translate them to a single public address for Internet connection.

3. There are two reasons for using NAT. First, it provides a level of security when your network is connected to the Internet. It hides the internal addresses of the network and restricts the services that can access the internal network. It also lets you conserve public IP addresses.

4. You've purchased one public IP address from the ISP along with the dedicated line. The only way your users can connect is to assign internal IP addresses to those computers. The Windows 2000 Server needs to have Routing and Remote Access enabled and configured as an Internet Connection Server to connect to the Internet link.

5. To monitor NAT, you would launch the Routing and Remote Access console. On the left window pane, right-click the NAT icon and select Statistics.

ANSWERS TO KEY TERM QUIZ

1. UDP
2. Request For Comments

3. Internet Connection Sharing
4. Private IP Address
5. Network Address Translation

11

Installing, Configuring, Managing, Monitoring, and Troubleshooting Certificate Services

T he present growth and interconnection of today's networks presents a challenge for today's administrators. This melding of networks increases a network's exposure to unauthorized access. To help ensure the integrity and privacy of transferred data, Windows 2000 provides a component named Microsoft Certificate Services.

In this chapter we'll look at Certificate Services and the type of encryption it provides. We'll install and configure an Enterprise root Certificate Authority. We'll manage and administer Certificates by managing a Certification Authority and Certificate snap-in with MMC. We'll renew a Certification Authority Certificate, and edit a default domain group policy object. We'll export certification private keys to provide added security, and lastly, identify what may cause Certificate errors.

LAB EXERCISE 11.01

Overview of Certificate Services

15 Minutes

The Cranston Brewing Company has a Windows 2000 domain that spans all five New England states. They have five domain controllers, eight member servers, and close to 900 Windows 2000 Professional workstations. You, as network engineer, want to implement Certificates as added security. How would you install Certification Authority for this enterprise?

Learning Objectives

Certificate Services use Certificates needed for a Private Key Infrastructure (PKI). PKI verifies and authenticates the validity of each client involved in an electronic transmission using Public Key Cryptography.

In this lab, you'll perform an installation of an Enterprise root CA for the company. These steps require several pre-installed services in order to function. By the end of this lab, you'll know how to:

■ Install and configure Certificate Services
■ Setup the Enterprise root Certification Authority (CA)

Lab Materials and Setup

This lab will require the following items:

- A working computer
- Installed network card
- Windows 2000 Server software
- Windows 2000 DNS service installed
- Windows 2000 AD service installed
- Windows 2000 IIS installed

lab
Hint *Users request Certificates through IIS.*

Getting Down to Business

To begin the installation and configuration of an Enterprise root CA, perform the following:

Step 1. Double-click Add/Remote Programs in the Control Panel. Click Add/Remove Windows Components in the dialog window.

Step 2. Select the Certificate Services option from the list and click Next.

lab
Warning *A warning appears stating that the computer cannot be named, added, or renamed from the domain after you add this service.*

Step 3. Click Yes to close the warning and click Next.

Step 4. Select the Enterprise root CA option in the Certificate Authority Type window. Click Next.

Step 5. The next window requires you to enter the information to identifying the Certificate Authority. Enter the following information:

- CA name: Payroll CA
- Organization: Southernbell

■ Organization unit: Payroll

■ City, State, Country: (fill in the appropriate location)

■ E-mail: paymaster@southernbell.com

■ CA description: Payroll CA Authority

■ The CA's validity date can be adjusted.

Step 6. Click Next. In the dialog window note the locations of the database and database logs. You need to enter the shared folder location for the configuration files.

lab
Hint

If Internet Information Services (IIS) is running, the wizard will need to stop the services. Click OK to let the wizard continue.

Step 7. Click Next and complete to complete the process.

LAB EXERCISE 11.02

Managing and Administering Certificates

15 Minutes

You are the consulting network engineer for Yankee Doodles, Ltd. Their newly installed Windows 2000 domain consists of eight domain controllers, five member servers, and 1,440 Windows 2000 Professional workstations. Certificate Services and an Enterprise root Certification Authority (CA) have been installed and configured. What's your next set of steps in the Certificate Services process?

Learning Objectives

Once the Certification Authority has been installed, it is necessary to install the Certificates and the Certificate Authority Snap-in. The Certificates manage the Certificates that the CA receives from other CAs in the enterprise. The CA manages policy settings, issued and revoked Certificates, and pending requests.

In this lab exercise you'll create a new MMC and add the Certificates snap-in and Certification Authority.

By the end of this lab, you will know how to:

■ Create an MMC for Certificate management

■ Add the Certificates snap-in

■ Add the Certificate Authority snap-in

Lab Material and Setup

This lab will require the following:

■ A working computer

■ Installed network card

■ Windows 2000 Server software

■ Windows 2000 DNS service installed

■ Windows 2000 AD service installed

■ Windows 2000 IIS installed

lab
⓵int   *Users request Certificates through IIS.*

Getting Down to Business

To create a new MMC console and add the Certification Authority and Certificates snap-in, perform the following:

Step 1.   Launch Microsoft Management Console.

Step 2.   Open the Add Standalone Snap-In dialog box from the Console. Click Add.

Step 3.   Add the Certification Authority snap-in. Verify that Local computer is selected in the dialog window. Click Finish.

Step 4.   Add the Certificates snap-in. In the Certificates snap-in dialog window choose Computer Account. Click Next.

Step 5.   Verify that Local is selected. Click Finish and complete the process.

Step 6.   Save your configuration and name the console Certificates.

Step 7.   Exit out of the Microsoft Management Console.

LAB EXERCISE 11.03

Creating and Issuing Certificates in Windows 2000

5 Minutes

You are a senior administrator for Mid-Atlantic Bank. Their Windows 2000 domain consists of fifteen domain controllers, ten member servers, and 1,500 Windows 2000 Professional workstations. Because of the bank's delicate and confidential customer information, the root Certification Authority's Certificates need to be renewed to maintain a high level of security. Perform the renew process.

Learning Objectives

A root CA includes a validity period. At the end of that period the Certificate is disabled. The program is set up so that when a root CA's own Certificate expires, so too the subordinate CAs that it issues to.

In this lab exercise you'll renew the root Certification Authority Certificates to ensure a secure enterprise. By the end of this lab, you will know how to:

■ Renew a root Certification Authority

Lab Materials and Setup

This lab will require the following:

■ A working computer
■ Installed network card
■ Windows 2000 Server software

■ Windows 2000 DNS service installed

■ Windows 2000 AD service installed

■ Windows 2000 IIS installed

lab
①int   *Users request Certificates through IIS.*

Getting Down to Business

To renew a root Certification Authority perform the following:

Step 1.   Start the Certificate Authority console.

Step 2.   Select the root CA and renew the CA Certificate.

Step 3.   Select Yes to generate a new public and private key. Click OK to complete the process.

LAB EXERCISE 11.04

Configuring Certificate-Based Authentication

15 Minutes

Your company, Big-bITe Consultants, has sent you to San Antonio, Texas to help South-of-the-Border Importers set up an auto enrollment policy for the company computers. The company, which imports food products from Mexico and South America, has a Windows 2000 network consisting of four domain controllers, two member servers, and 360 Windows 2000 Professional workstations. You've been at this company once before at the beginning of the year to set up their DNS.

Learning Objectives

Automatic Certificate requests for computers allow the administrator to request Certificates from the Certification Authorities for computers receiving the auto-enrollment Group Policy.

In this lab exercise, you'll edit the Domain Group Policy and configure an auto-enrollment policy. By the end of this lab, you will know how to:

■ Edit the Default Domain Policy Group Policy Object (GPO)

■ Launch the Automatic Certificate Request Wizard

■ Create the automatic Certificate request

Lab Materials and Setup

This lab will require the following:

■ A working computer

■ Installed network card

■ Windows 2000 Server software

■ Windows 2000 DNS service installed

■ Windows 2000 AD service installed

■ Windows 2000 IIS installed

lab
(i)int   *Users request Certificates through IIS.*

Getting Down to Business

To create an Auto-Enrollment Policy for Computers perform the following:

Step 1.   Launch the Microsoft Management Console.

Step 2.   Add the Active Directory Users and Computers snap-in management component to the Console using Add/Remove Snap-in.

Step 3.   Expand Active Directory Users and Computers and edit the Default Domain Policy Group Policy Object, select Properties for Southernbell.com. In the properties dialog window click the Group Policy tab and edit the Default Domain Policy.

Step 4.   The Group Policy management console opens. Now you need to launch the Automatic Certificate Request Setup wizard. Find and right-click Automatic Certificate Request Settings and select New. Start the Automatic Certificate Request wizard.

Step 5.   Perform the wizard steps and complete the Certificate Template process.

LAB EXERCISE 11.05

15 Minutes

Encrypting File System (EFS) Recovery Keys

The Golden Grain Agricultural Services has a Windows 2000 domain that spans six mid-western states. The company has seven Windows 2000 domain controllers, four member servers, and close to 1,100 Windows 2000 Professional workstations. Fully 350 of those Windows 2000 workstations are installed onto laptops. Your concern as a systems engineer is the use of laptops with sensitive information. What would happen if the laptops were stolen or lost? Could the information be jeopardized?

Learning Objectives

The solution here is to remove the EFS Recovery Keys. EFS is one of the best data security tools for laptop users. Removing the EFS keys and placing them on a floppy disk will prevent an intruder from gaining access to that information.

In this lab exercise, you'll export the EFS Keys to a floppy disk. By the end of this lab, you will know how to:

- Add the Group Policy snap-in
- Export the recovery keys
- Remove the default key from the local computer

Lab Materials and Setup

This lab will require the following:

- A working computer
- Installed network card
- Windows 2000 Server software
- Windows 2000 DNS service installed
- Windows 2000 AD service installed
- Windows 2000 IIS installed

lab
Hint   *Users request Certificates through IIS.*

Getting Down to Business

To Remove the EFS Recovery Key perform the following:

Step 1.   Launch the Microsoft Management Console.

Step 2.   Add the Group Policy snap-in list in the Console. Verify that Local Computer is in Group Policy Object. Click Finish and complete the process.

Step 3.   Now you are ready to export the recovery keys. Find and expand Public Key Policies.

Step 4.   Click the Encrypted Data Recovery Agents item and then right-click Administrator Select All Tasks and then click on Export.

Step 6.   Follow the dialog windows to export the Private Keys. Enter **a:\admincert** as the file name.

Step 7.   Lastly, you need to remove the default recovery key from the local computer. Right-click Administrator select All Tasks and then click on Delete. Click Yes for the warning message.

Step 8.   Close Console1 and click No to saving the Console1 settings.

LAB EXERCISE 11.06

Troubleshooting Certificates

10 Minutes

Frank is the new junior administrator in the company. It's been your task over the past three months to be his mentor. You've been able to present just about every aspect and component of a Windows 2000 system. This past week he's been reading a chapter in a training book about Certification Authorizations and Certificates issued by CAs. During a conversation he asks you about troubleshooting Certificates, and how they could cause problems. You mention that there are several conditions that contribute to the "delinquency" of a Certificate. You disclose three main conditions that would cause problems.

Learning Objectives

Certificates are sent with data verifying the authenticity of the sender. Certificates issued by the Certification Authority may at times become nonfunctioning. Understanding the common causes is essential for troubleshooting an uncooperative Certificate.

In this lab you'll identify common causes that contribute to uncooperative Certificates. By the end of this lab, you will know how to:

- Understand and explain Certificate problems
- Identify problem sources

Lab Materials and Setup

For this lab exercise, you'll need:

- Pencil and paper
- Windows 2000 Server

Getting Down to Business

Certificates can cause problems and concerns. Explore those in this exercise.

Step 1. List and describe the three most common problems associated with Certificates.

_____

_____

_____

_____

_____

_____

For help answering this question, refer to the section on "Troubleshooting Certificates" in Chapter 11 of the **Windows 2000 Network Administration Study Guide**.

LAB ANALYSIS TEST

1. You are the LAN administrator for a Windows 2000 network that consists of eight domain controllers. Additionally, there are two member servers and 751 Windows 2000 Professional workstations. Your network spans three cities: San Francisco, Montgomery, and St Louis. Due to the recent events with network volatility, you would like to implement Certificates as an additional security step. Your IT manager wants to know why you'd like to implement Certificates. Explain.

   _____

   _____

2. Your IT manager also wants to know what a Certificate Authority is and what role does the subordinate CA play. What will you tell him?

   _____

   _____

3. You've successfully installed your Enterprise root CA and subordinate CA. Additionally; you want to secure the CA Certificate to prevent a possible loss. How would you ensure that the private encryption key is backed up?

   _____

   _____

4. Some members of your client base at your company use laptops to connect to the network. One of your concerns is the security of those laptops if they lost or stolen. How effective can EFS be to help with this potential occurrence?

   _____

   _____

5. Roberta is installing a Certificate Authority on a Windows 2000 Server. The CA will be responding to requests submitted over the Internet. Active Directory will not handle requests for authentication. What type of CA does Roberta need to install?

   _____

   _____

KEY TERM QUIZ

Use the following vocabulary terms to complete the sentences below. Not all of the terms will be used.

>   Public Key Certificate
>
>   Public Key Infrastructure
>
>   Encrypting File System
>
>   Certificate
>
>   Standalone Certification Authorities
>
>   validity period
>
>   One-to-One Certificate Mapping
>
>   Many-to-One Certificate Mapping
>
>   Certificate Authority
>
>   Digital Signature

1. _____ is a credential used to authenticate origin and identity of the public part of a public/private key pair. This Certificate ensures that the transmitted data is kept secure.

2. A way for the sender of a message, file, or other data to bind their identity to the information is named a/an _____.

3. The term generally used to describe the laws, policies, standards and software that regulate Certificates, public and private keys, is named _____.

4. Windows 2000 uses the _____ to allow users to encode files and folders on an NTFS volume to prevent intruder from viewing or gaining access to them.

5. A service named _____ is responsible for the authenticity of public keys that belong to users. One of the ways this is done is through digitally signed Certificates.

LAB WRAP-UP

In this chapter we looked at Certificate Services and the type of encryption it provides. By securing data using some type of encryption, it prevents anyone from decoding that data. We saw that encryption keys have two parts to them, a public key that is distributed to users and a private key that stays on the server. We worked with managing and administering Certificates, creating and issuing Certificates through the use of the Certificate Authority Management Console snap-in. We also worked with Encrypting File System (EFS), a system that uses Public Key Infrastructure (PKI)-based security. And lastly, we looked at troubleshooting common Certificate problems.

LAB SOLUTIONS FOR CHAPTER 11

Lab Solution 11.01

Certificate Services use Certificates needed for a Private Key Infrastructure (PKI). PKI verifies and authenticates the validity of each client involved in an electronic transmission using Public Key Cryptography.

In this lab, you perform an installation of an Enterprise root CA for the company. These steps require several pre-installed services in order to function. By the end of this lab, you'll be able to:

■ Install and configure Certificate Services

■ Setup the Enterprise root Certification Authority (CA)

To begin the installation and configuration of an Enterprise root CA, perform the following:

Step 1. Click Start | Settings | Control Panel

Step 2. Double-click Add/Remove Programs. In the dialog box that opens, click Add/Remove Windows Components. The Windows Components Wizard opens with a list of components.

Step 3. Select the Certificate Services option as shown in Figure 11-1, and click Next.

lab
Warning   *A warning appears stating that the computer cannot be named, added, or removed from the domain after you add this service.*

Step 4. Click Yes to close the warning and click Next.

Step 5. In the Certificate Authority Type window, select the Enterprise root CA option as shown in Figure 11-2. Click Next.

Add Certificate
Services using the
Windows
Components
Wizard

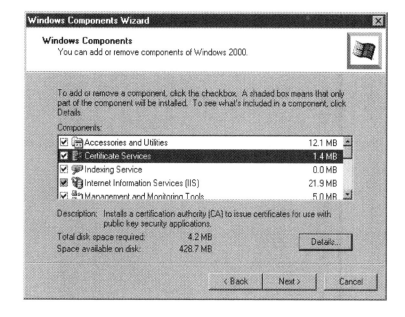

Other Certificate
Authorities are
chosen from this
window

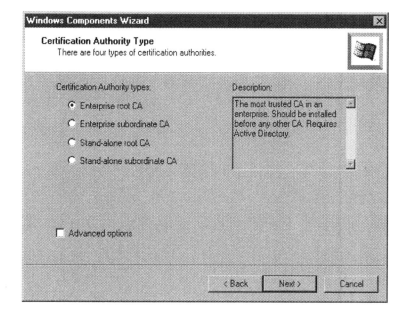

Step 6. The next window requires you to enter the information to identifying the Certificate Authority. Enter the following information:

- CA name: Payroll CA
- Organization: Southernbell
- Organization unit: Payroll
- City, State, Country (fill-in the appropriate location)
- E-mail: paymaster@southernbell.com
- CA description: Payroll CA Authority
- The CA's validity date can be adjusted.

Step 7. Click Next. The Data Storage Location dialog window opens. Note the locations of the database and database logs. You need to enter the shared folder location for the configuration files as shown in Figure 11-3.

If Internet Information Services (IIS) is running, the wizard will need to stop the services. Click OK to let the wizard continue.

FIGURE 11-3

Optional storage locations can be configured in this window

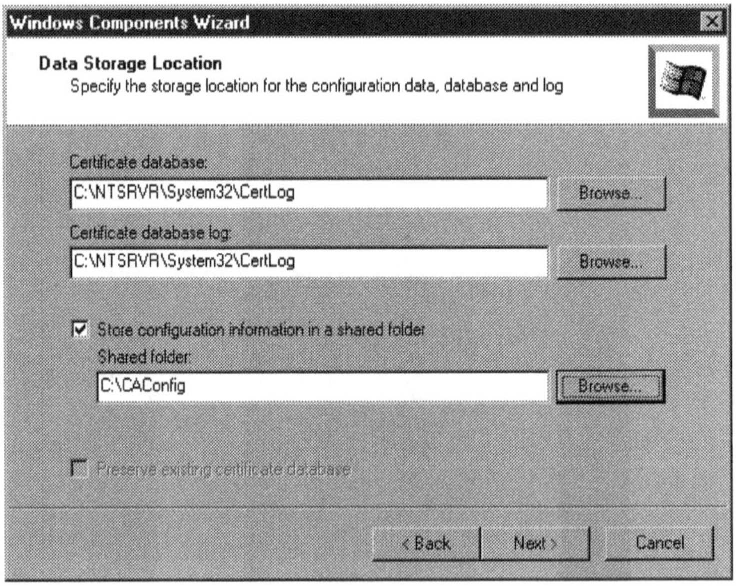

Step 8. Click Next to complete the process. The wizard copies the necessary files to the Windows 2000 Server. Click Finish to exit.

Lab Solution 11.02

Once the Certification Authority has been installed, it is necessary to install the Certificates and the Certificate Authority snap-in. The CA manages policy settings, issued and revoked Certificates, and pending requests.

In this lab exercise you'll create a new MMC and add the Certificates snap-in and Certification Authority.

By the end of this lab, you'll be able to:

■ Create an MMC for Certificate management

■ Add the Certificates snap-in

■ Add the Certificate Authority snap-in

To create a new MMC console and add the Certification Authority and Certificates snap-in, perform the following:

Step 1. Click Start | Run. In the Run field type mmc, click the OK button.

Step 2. Click Console from the menu and select Add/Remove Snap-in from the menu options and click Add. The Add Standalone Snap-In dialog window opens.

Step 3. Select Certification Authority, and click Add. In the Certification Authority dialog box that opens, verify that Local computer is selected as shown in Figure 11-4. Click Finish.

Step 4. Select Certificates from the list and click Add. In the Certificates snap-in dialog window choose Computer Account as shown in Figure 11-5. Click Next.

Step 5. In the next window, verify that Local is selected. Click Finish to complete the process. Close the Add Snap-In dialog window and then click OK.

FIGURE 11-4

Select the
computer that will
manage the
Certification
Authority

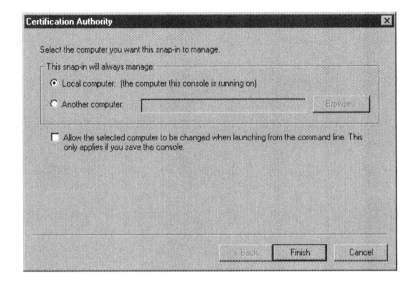

Step 6. To save your configuration, Click Console and select Save. The Save As dialog window opens. Name the console Certificates and click Save.

Step 7. Exit out of the Microsoft Management Console.

FIGURE 11-5

The snap-in will
also manage the
Computer
Account

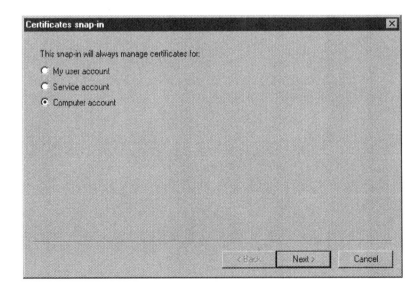

Lab Solution 11.03

A root CA includes a validity period. At the end of that period the Certificate is disabled. The program is set up so that when a root CA's own Certificate expires so too the subordinate CAs that it issues to.

In this lab exercise you'll renew the root Certification Authority Certificates to ensure a secure enterprise. By the end of this lab, you'll be able to:

- Renew a root Certification Authority

To renew a root Certification Authority perform the following:

Step 1. Click Start | Programs | Administrative Tools | Certificate Authority.

Step 2. Select the root CA and click Action from the menu. Select Action | All Tasks| Renew CA Certificate. The Renew CA Certificate dialog window opens. This window also gives you the option to consider generating a new signing key.

Step 3. Select Yes to generate a new public and private key. Click OK to complete the process.

Lab Solution 11.04

Automatic Certificate requests for computers allow the administrator to request Certificates from the Certification Authorities for computers receiving the auto-enrollment Group Policy.

In this lab exercise, you'll edit the Domain Group Policy and configure an auto-enrollment policy. By the end of this lab, you'll be able to:

- Edit the Default Domain Policy Group Policy Object (GPO)
- Launch the Automatic Certificate Request Wizard
- Create the automatic Certificate request

To create an Auto-Enrollment Policy for Computers perform the following:

Step 1. Click Start | Run. In the Run field type **mmc**, click the OK button.

Step 2.   With Console root selected in the left windowpane, click Console from the menu. From the menu select Add/Remove Snap-in. Through this utility, you need to add the Active Directory Users and Computers management component as shown in Figure 11-6.

Step 3.   In the Add/Remove Snap-in dialog window click Add. From the available Snap-in list click Active Directory Users and Computers. Click Add, then click Close.

Step 4.   In the left windowpane, expand Active Directory Users and Computers. To edit the Default Domain Policy Group Policy Object, right-click Southernbell.com, select Properties. In the properties dialog window click the Group Policy tab. Within the window, click Default Domain Policy and click Edit as shown in Figure 11-7.

Step 5.   The Group Policy management console opens. Now you need to launch the Automatic Certificate Request Setup wizard. Expand Computer Configuration in the left windowpane, expand Windows Settings, Security Settings, and then Public Key Policies. Now, right-click Automatic Certificate Request Settings and select New. Click Automatic Certificate Request as shown in Figure 11-8. Click Next to start the wizard.

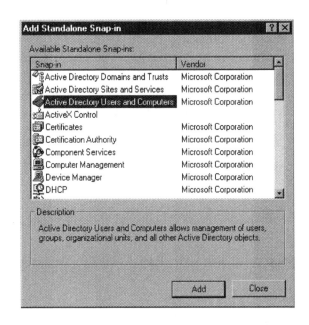

FIGURE 11-6

Add the Active Directory Users and Computers management

FIGURE 11-7

Edit the Default Domain Policy object to define user and computer configurations

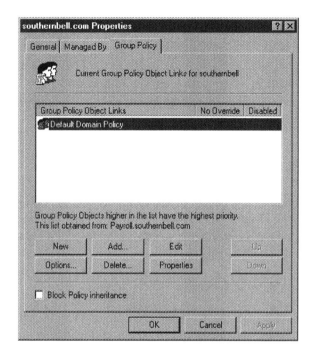

FIGURE 11-8

Add a new Automatic Certificate Request object to the Security Settings

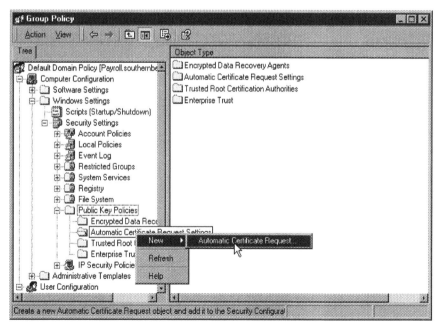

Step 6. In the Certificate Template window select Computer as shown in Figure 11-9. Click Next.

Step 7. Select the Certificate Authority, Payroll CA, to automate the Certificate request. Click Next then Finish to complete the process. Click OK in the properties dialog window.

Lab Solution 11.05

The solution here is to remove the EFS Recovery Keys. EFS is one of the best data security tools for laptop users. Removing the EFS keys and placing them on a floppy disk will prevent an intruder from gaining access to that information.

In this lab exercise, you'll export the EFS Keys to a floppy disk. By the end of this lab, you'll be able to:

- Add the Group Policy snap-in
- Export the recovery keys
- Remove the default key from the local computer

Select the Computer Certificate template that has preset authentication parameters in place

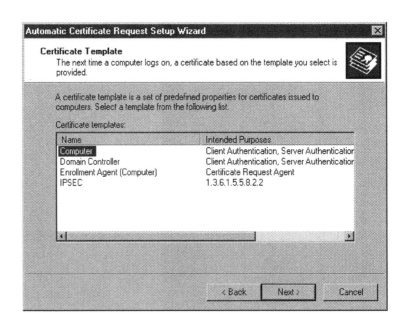

To Remove the EFS Recovery Key perform the following:

Step 1. First, you need to add the Group Policy Snap-in in MMC. Click Start | Run. In the Run field type **mmc**, click the OK button.

Step 2. Click the Console menu item, select and click Add/Remove Snap-in. In the Add/Remove Snap-in dialog window click Add. From the Snap-in list select Group Policy as shown in Figure 11-10. Click Add.

Step 3. Verify that Local Computer is in Group Policy Object. Click Finish to complete the process. Click Close in the snap-in dialog window, then click OK.

Step 4. Now you are ready to export the recovery keys. Expand Local Computer Policy in the left windowpane of Console. Expand Computer Configuration, Windows Settings, Security Settings, and lastly, Public Key Policies.

Select the Group Policy object to edit with the MMC

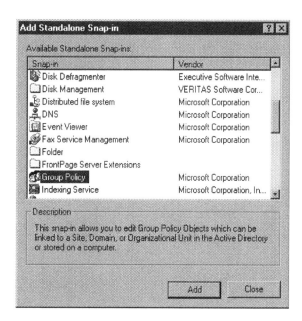

Step 5. Click the Encrypted Data Recovery Agents item in the left windowpane. Right-click Administrator in the right windowpane. Select All Tasks and then click on Export as shown in Figure 11-11.

Step 6. Click Next in the Export Private Key window. Click Next in the Export File System window. In the File to Export window enter **a:\admincert** as the file name as shown in Figure 11-12.

Step 7. Lastly, you need to remove the default recovery key from the local computer. Right-click Administrator in the right windowpane again. Select All Tasks and then click Delete. Click Yes for the warning message.

Step 8. Close Console1 and click No to saving the Console1 settings.

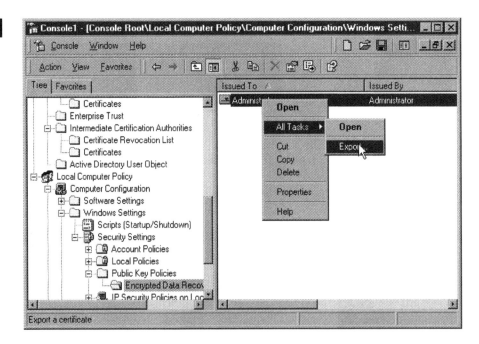

FIGURE 11-11

Select the Certificate issued to the Administrator account for export

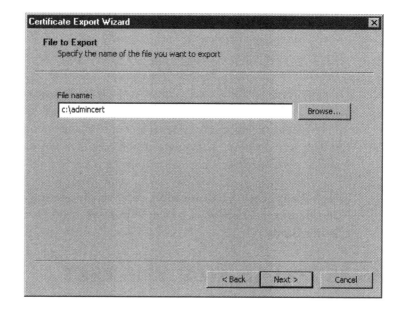

Lab Solution 11.06

Certificates are sent with data verifying the authenticity of the sender. Certificates by the Certification Authority may, at times, become nonfunctioning. Understanding the common causes is essential for troubleshooting an un-cooperating Certificate.

In this lab you'll identify common causes that contribute to un-cooperating Certificates. By the end of this lab, you'll be able to:

- Understand and explain Certificate problems
- Identify problem sources

What are the three most common problems associated with Certificates?

Step 1.   Delinquent Certificates can be caused by several factors. Here we'll list three common ones. The first cause of delinquent Certificates is corrupt data. These errors can occur from data transmission, a software bug, or loss of connection during Certificate creation or transfer. This can cause a bad password or a misguided path to the account information. To solve this type of problem you would need to check the password for that account, and verify that the content of the Certificate is correct.

A second cause is an invalid request format. This means that the request could not be interpreted properly, or is incorrectly processed. You would need to verify the contents of the Certificate, looking at the properties and intent of the Certificate. The solution would include the re-creation of the Certificate.

Additionally, a third cause is incorrect Certificate mapping. Here, the information in the Certificate is pointing to the incorrect user or computer account. This type of problem is usually discovered when a user or computer account has been short-changed of their security level. The only solution here is to replace the present Certificate with a new Certificate.

For help answering this question, refer to the section on Troubleshooting Certificates in Chapter 11 of the **Windows 2000 Network Administration Study Guide***.*

ANSWERS TO LAB ANALYSIS TEST

1. A Certificate is a component of Windows 2000 that allows secure data transmission over a network. A digital signature is attached, so to speak, that assures the receiver that the sender is who he or she claims to be. It also assures the sender that the data will reach the recipient without compromise. You can add Certificate services as part of Windows 2000.

2. A CA is an entity responsible for verifying the credentials of a Certificate requestor prior to giving the requestor a Certificate. It is considered an electronic password or user identification. It proves that you are who you are. Once verified, you are allowed access to resources and information. A subordinate CA is responsible for issuing Certificates to child CAs. The Enterprise root CA issues a Certificate to the subordinate CA that in turn issues Certificates to end-users and computers.

For more information, refer to the section on Certificate Authority in Chapter 11 of the **Windows 2000 Network Administration Study Guide***.*

3. To back up your private encryption key you would export the CA Certificate with the Certificate Export wizard to copy the Certificate to another folder on the system. In addition, backing up system state data on a Certificate server backs up the Certificates.

4. Quite basically, when EFS is used on a laptop, you need to export the private keys and delete the recovery keys. This secures the data should the laptop be lost or stolen. Being bound to the users, the private encryption keys will only expose the data if the users themselves log in.

5. Roberta will be installing a stand-alone subordinate CA. It operates as a solitary Certificate that is used when issuing Certificates.

ANSWERS TO KEY TERM QUIZ

1. Certificate

2. digital signature

3. public key infrastructure

4. encrypting file system

5. Certificate Authority

INDEX

INTERNATIONAL CONTACT INFORMATION

AUSTRALIA
McGraw-Hill Book Company Australia Pty. Ltd.
TEL +61-2-9417-9899
FAX +61-2-9417-5687
http://www.mcgraw-hill.com.au
books-it_sydney@mcgraw-hill.com

CANADA
McGraw-Hill Ryerson Ltd.
TEL +905-430-5000
FAX +905-430-5020
http://www.mcgrawhill.ca

GREECE, MIDDLE EAST,
NORTHERN AFRICA
McGraw-Hill Hellas
TEL +30-1-656-0990-3-4
FAX +30-1-654-5525

MEXICO (Also serving Latin America)
McGraw-Hill Interamericana Editores S.A. de C.V.
TEL +525-117-1583
FAX +525-117-1589
http://www.mcgraw-hill.com.mx
fernando_castellanos@mcgraw-hill.com

SINGAPORE (Serving Asia)
McGraw-Hill Book Company
TEL +65-863-1580
FAX +65-862-3354
http://www.mcgraw-hill.com.sg
mghasia@mcgraw-hill.com

SOUTH AFRICA
McGraw-Hill South Africa
TEL +27-11-622-7512
FAX +27-11-622-9045
robyn_swanepoel@mcgraw-hill.com

UNITED KINGDOM & EUROPE
(Excluding Southern Europe)
McGraw-Hill Education Europe
TEL +44-1-628-502500
FAX +44-1-628-770224
http://www.mcgraw-hill.co.uk
computing_neurope@mcgraw-hill.com

ALL OTHER INQUIRIES Contact:
Osborne/McGraw-Hill
TEL +1-510-549-6600
FAX +1-510-883-7600
http://www.osborne.com
omg_international@mcgraw-hill.com

New Offerings from Osborne's
How to Do Everything Series

How to Do Everything with Your Palm™ Handheld, 2nd Edition
ISBN: 0-07-219100-7
Available: Now

How to Do Everything with Your Scanner
ISBN: 0-07-219106-6
Available: Now

How to Do Everything with Your Visor, 2nd Edition
ISBN: 0-07-219392-1
Available: October 2001

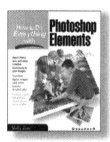

How to Do Everything with Photoshop Elements
ISBN: 0-07-219184-8
Available: September 2001

How to Do Everything with Your Blackberry
ISBN: 0-07-219393-X
Available: October 2001

How to Do Everything with Digital Video
ISBN: 0-07-219463-4
Available: November 2001

How to Do Everything with MP3 and Digital Music
ISBN: 0-07-219413-8
Available: December 2001

How to Do Everything with Your Web Phone
ISBN: 0-07-219412-X
Available: January 2002

How to Do Everything with Your iMac, 3rd Edition
ISBN: 0-07-213172-1
Available: October 2001

HTDE with Your Pocket PC & Handheld PC
ISBN: 07-212420-2
Available: Now

www.ingramcontent.com/pod-product-compliance
Lightning Source LLC
Chambersburg PA
CBHW080355060326
40689CB00019B/4014